THE PRICE INDEX

THE PRICE INDEX

S.N. AFRIAT

CAMBRIDGE UNIVERSITY PRESS

Cambridge

London : New York : Melbourne

Published by the Syndics of the Cambridge University Press
The Pitt Building, Trumpington Street, Cambridge CB2 1RP
Bentley House, 200 Euston Road, London NW1 2DB
32 East 57th Street, New York, NY 10022, USA
296 Beaconsfield Parade, Middle Park, Melbourne 3206, Australia

First published 1977

Printed in Great Britain by
Kingprint Ltd., Richmond, Surrey

Library of Congress Cataloguing in Publication Data

Afriat, S   N   1925–

The price index.

Bibliography: p.

1. Price indexes. I. Title.
HB225.A33 1977   339.4'2   77–2134
ISBN 0 521 21665 6

CONTENTS

FIGURES

To
Alan Brown, Richard Stone, Robin Marris
with whom this started
Oskar Morgenstern
with whom it was finished
and
Edgar O. Edwards
who ordered retreat
to the beginning
again

PREFACE

With the usual diagram (tea on one axis and coffee on the other), Alan
Brown explained the cost-of-living adjustment of an income in response to
a price change, my first day at the Department of Applied Economics,
Cambridge, in 1953. I could not see what this had to do with a price
index and how it could possibly be resolved by the use of one, as it usually
is. Our work with Professor J.R.N. Stone in demand analysis fixed an
interest in the subject. H. Houthakker had been visiting the year before
and his "revealed preference" paper was circulating, spreading that
influence. Robin Marris introduced the Laspeyres and Paasche indices and
the question of their "spread", and told me of Buscheguennce's remark about
Fisher's index. The communication now makes the subject of this book. At
that time it prompted a non-homogeneous extension of Fisher's formula
involving four periods simultaneously which, from a remark of Houthakker
a few years later, turned out also to be an extension of Wald's "New Formula".
This was the start also of other inquiries which have effect in the methods
but are not otherwise dealt with here.

Attention to index questions which started then, even on that first
day, continued when I went to work with Professor Oskar Morgenstern at the
Econometric Research Program, Princeton, in 1958. The concern there was
with generalizations which, as seemed natural, should involve demand data
from any number of periods simultaneously and do away with price indices.
When I reported this work in a lecture at Rice University in 1962, Edgar
Edwards said an exposition of it ought to be given showing how it applied

to price indices in the usual context of just two periods. I agreed and
this, after a fair lapse of time, is the result.

A summary account of the further theory depending on the same approach
has been published (NBER 1970 Conference), showing the main ideas, without details of the arguments. Parts which affect the present work have
had no exposition other than in the early research reports; the bibliography here lists these and related material which is available. That
account touches on the price index in theory and practice, and on the
essential limitation of the idea and a particular line of retreat from it.
This is a retreat requiring its own report, but an appendix here offers
a simple practical result.

There can be hesitation in offering a work which is without dependence
on empiricism as a contribution to any kind of economic knowledge. But
price indices are everywhere in economic thinking and statistics. Also,
economic thinking makes a powerful part of economic reality. The meaning
of "price level" may give no concern in well known spheres of theory
where, by the nature of them, form itself is an essential substance and a
main support, and is maintained with almost blameless fidelity. But outside
those there is a less ready submission.

Much rests on the "price index" in theory and in practice, and that
alone makes desirable a crystallization of what is involved. Outstanding
questions are better exhausted because otherwise the subject retains
importance, and it is not greatly interesting, whatever its internal
fascinations, since it deals with an instrument of perception and not with
any perception. With all the attention the subject has received, it still
has obscurities. The teaching of it puzzles students and anyone unaccustomed

to the gestures of argument which take place with a lack of necessary
definitions.

The result intended now is to give an explicit sense to very familiar
terms and statements, not actually to repudiate them. Especially there
is recognition, absent in most teaching, that "price index" is an entirely
"homogeneous" idea. Against that is the knowledge that things in economic
reality are thoroughly unhomogeneous — but that is another matter.

The index problem, which has been taken up with interest at times and
dropped with exhaustion or boredom at others, is always present, and it
has usually been taken up during times of inflation. There is now a widespread questioning about the adequacy of the price index for its practical
purposes. Inflation brings attention to price indices but on its own does
not necessarily damage their reputation. Now it is an additional influence
which is present, which has been described by Professor Ralf Dahrendorf
in the 1974 Reith Lectures. This has bearing because a price index, in
the theoretical notion a ratio of "price-levels", is constructed statistically as some kind of average of price-ratios. He says: "...the end of
expansion is also the end of the average." "At a time of general expansion,
average figures gave some indication of a trend felt by most." "...such
averages are now losing much of their meaning." "The end of the average
means that much more attention will have to be given to differences..."

Obviously the impact of a price change on anyone depends entirely on
what they want to buy. Purchasing habits vary widely, especially when
there are widely different incomes. Thus in spite of the implication of a
price index that the impact — understood as proportional adjustment of
income to offset the effect on purchasing power of the price change — is

the same everywhere, it is in principle, and in reality, different where
income and equally anything else is different. No one would care so much
about this variation when most incomes are rising in purchasing power.
But in contrary circumstances "...much more attention will have to be
given to differences...". It should no longer be plausible, even to the
most habitual "price level" theoreticians, that the whole situation can
be effectively summarized by a single number. It never has been plausible,
even though prodigious theories have depended on the idea. It has been
tolerable only because it did not matter.

Acknowledgements of debts scattered over many years for an altogether
small work offered finally in what seems to be the twilight of its subject,
and salvaged from a heap of material going round interests mainly its own,
which I have often been reminded is not in the manner for economists,
could inflate the matter too much but for the agreeable recollection of
them.

Some of these will already be evident, but I want to mention Professor
Morgenstern with affectionate thanks for sponsoring the work in Princeton
during 1958-1962, and for his friendship.

Also I wish to give acknowledgement to the U.S. National Science
Foundation and to the National Research Council of Canada for support of
projects in consumer theory of which this is part.

Finally, there is one to Bridget Carruthers, who typed it.

Ottawa   S.N.A.
March 1975

POSTSCRIPT to PREFACE

Additions to the original manuscript consist in the Introductions and
the computations in the Appendix. I acknowledge with thanks my indebt-
edness to John Kuiper, my collaborator and colleague at the University
of Ottawa, for his work with the computations. They are a part of a
Report delivered to the Economic Council of Canada for a study on
Consumers' Expenditures and Inflation sponsored jointly with Departments
of the Government of Canada; they are reproduced here with permission of
the Economic Council of Canada.

A preliminary to this study was carried out with partial support from
the Canada Council. It has benefited from consultations with
Mr. W.M. Illing, Director of the Prices Division, and the helpful cooper-
ation of others at Statistics Canada. Also I have had valuable discussion
with Mr. E.J. van Goudoever of Health and Welfare Canada, especially
concerning the incremental inflation rate. That idea is not accountable
in "price index" terms, and is a counter-point to the habitual thinking
in those terms.

Though the incremental price index, and its statistical counterpart
which measures incremental inflation rates, is new as a concept (and
needs to be distinguished from the marginal price index idea which has
been used by this and other writers, which has reference to a particular
utility function) an instance of it comes out of algebraical rearrangement
in the "New Formula" of Wald (1939). The data for the formula are a pair
of expansion loci which are general lines in the commodity space, and

the result is a general linear relation between incomes which, at the
respective prices, have the same purchasing power. The incremental
price index is given by the slope of the relation. The formula for this
"incremental" index is identical with Fisher's price index except that
bundles of goods are replaced by "incremental bundles", that is, dis-
placements on the expansion lines specifying their directions. The
Laspeyres and Paasche price indices similarly have "incremental" analogues
based on the same data. All these are no different from price indices
in the "homogeneous" case when the expansion lines are rays through the
origin and correspondingly the relation between equivalent incomes is
one of simple proportionality. A theory of incremental price indices
parallel to the theory of price indices has been outlined elsewhere
(Afriat Aug. 1961, Aug. 1970 and NBER 1970 Conference). Statistical
counterparts are the inflation rate (CPI) and incremental rate, the latter
being the same as the former only in case of there being a suitable
"homogeneity". Comparison of the two rates gives basis for a measurement
of "inflation bias". These various statistics are explained and illustrated especially in the Appendix. To give a systematic account of
these further ideas is not the purpose now; they need a separate treatment.
They are brought in to give an enlargement around the price index which
illustrates the limitation of that idea and also an escape.

My acknowledgements would be incomplete without mention of unaccountable
benefits from conversations with W.M. Gorman, of the London School of
Economics, at intervals over many years. He is the only person I know
with whom any matter here could always be talked about instantly, with
unfailing mercuric readiness; in particular, features of the "marginal"

matter which has a place in this book were already very much an old
subject with him.

In a final pursuit of the True Index and under the mistaken impression
that the Guardian of it was a complete stranger, I am glad to have found
Findlay Forsyth, of the Department of Employment and my colleague and
friend at the D.A.E. twenty years ago. An influence from our meeting is
in the discussion shown in Section 3 of the Introduction. Of course, he
has no responsibility for my probably having mixed up what he told me, or
for my encouragement from the impression of his not disagreeing with some
remarks.

It could seem from the 'camera-ready' production that this is — like
work of a pavement artist — all my own work. But members of the Staff at
the Cambridge University Press have had much influence in it. Cogent
suggestions, and restraints, moulded the enlargements made around the
originally offered material, and a merciless attention to detail has been
matched by a readiness to take advantage of it.

The readiness would have been futile had it not been on the part of
Paddye Kearney Mann, who assisted with the additional part of the manuscript,
Bridget Carruthers who returned to the typescript she started — apparently
so well as to leave no necessity for printers' type — and Kerry-Lynne Wilson
who with a metamorphosis of design completed it. We are indebted to the
National Research Council of Canada and to the Canada Council for support
and facilities which enabled the work to be done.

Ottawa   S.N.A.
December 1976

INTRODUCTION : THEORY AND PRACTICE

1. Comparisons

There is a dilemma in the comparison of two periods of time: they must have comparable features to bring them into a relation with each other at all, but also there is an essential separation so it is difficult to know what finally to make of the comparison. Philosophers in 10th Century Spain offered a simple view: the world is created afresh at every moment... This is certainly one way to abolish problems of comparison and connection. However, others, historians, economists or anybody else, believe things are not always so new: they dwell on connections, debts. In the other extreme, the only authority for the present is the past. In early economics the correct price or wage is simply the price or wage that has been settled by custom and has the value which, so far as anybody can remember, it has always had. No doubt this is not as senseless as it might immediately seem from the standpoint of neoclassical economics. But it presupposes moral order, obedience to norms. There can be no price cutting, and no charging of unexpectedly high prices. This makes sense in a steady way of life where supply and demand have created each other and settled down together. Whatever the limitations of this way of thinking which limit its current scope, it is at least completely rational. Walras pursues the opposite situation in a logical way, but at the same time he helps foster a myth, which we have also from Adam Smith. However with Smith it is not a deliberate and indispensable truth to be pursued with trappings of exact science. From him it can appear as an archaic phantasy, inadvertantly inherited from predecessors. In the alternative system, which is more familiar to us at least intellectually, price cutting and boosting is permitted freely, there is no law but competition, but out of this competition emerges *the optimal result*.

Here is not really a proposition that something — it is not said or known what — is at a maximum. It is an exhortation which connects, better than with anything in the differential calculus, with the 10th Century philosopher: the Walrasian economy is always newly at its best at any moment. There can be no argument that it should be any different. Therefore it is pointless to do accounts which compare one moment with another. But standing out in practice is the opposite, familiarly old attitude, which is that the past has authority for the present. Price indices express respect for that authority. They offer a kind of exchange-rate between $$ in different periods; accounts in one period can be converted to show them as if they were accounts in another period, and then they can be compared with corresponding accounts in that other period. In particular, wages can be compared. A force acting on what a wage should be this year is what it was in some former year converted into this year's $$. Sums today are measured by a yardstick which has reference to the past. The "index number problem" can be understood as the problem of fashioning such a yardstick. There is a dilemma, because the present has to be placed in the past, but the present has a separation from the past which erases reference marks which could assist in the positioning. There are calibration difficulties. Different approaches to the problem are distinguished by the choice of calibrating instruments.

A price index signifies a special form of instrument whereby prices, though they are many, have a "level" in any period. Exchange rates between periods are then ratios of price levels, these being determined by "price indices". But this only gives a form and does not tell how it is to be realized, nor why such a simplistic form should be suitable.

A change through time can be recognized only by means of some element which persists unchanged. Thus if a material body is undergoing deformation in time, this can be known only by means of a measuring rod which is transported through time without deformation. With a price index which measures change in the "level" of prices there is dependence on a hypothetically unchanged construction, a special type of utility function. This function could be a very simple one determined from a single bundle of goods. This would be the case with a practical price index like the Consumer Price Index used in North America. But no purpose is served by bringing in utility functions at all in this case. Utility functions give service in theoretical discussions where they contribute structure which is an essential part of the matter. But the data used in practice cannot bear that structure.

Practice can stand without theory; put in another way, it con-stitutes its own theory. All that is accomplished by expressing anything in practice in terms of utility theory is to show it does not conflict with that theory. Practice is consistent with a poor specialization of that theory, so poor that nothing is added by bringing it in.

When prices change, from one period to another, purchases made in one period at a certain cost have a different cost in the other. Should prices all rise so will that cost. If a wage does not increase enough to meet the extra cost, sacrifices have to be made and living-style suffers. The work done in a job might remain the same but the return received from it in terms of ability to purchase wanted goods becomes less. The unsettling effects are familiar. Agitation takes place everywhere for incomes and all payments to increase. It becomes important to have a general basis for deciding the amount of any such increase. The experience of rising prices therefore creates the social need to have an accepted yardstick for judging the modifications due to incomes and other payments which would compensate them for the effects of price increases.

In common practice it is a "price index" which has use for such judgements. This is a number issued regularly from a government office which has official standing in the community as a description of how prices have changed in a given period. In Canada the Consumer Price Index or CPI has this role, and practices in other countries are similar. But there is a need served, reflected in the variety of uses, and then there are questions which feature in public discussions about whether this is fulfilled "adequately". The sense of such adequacy and how any question about it can be answered is not an altogether simple matter but has separate aspects. Two broad aspects, which encompass others, are about the character of the original statistical data, and then what is done with that data for whatever purpose. Interest here is in the second of these aspects, especially in the question whether the extraction of a single number, the "price index", from the available data is all that should be done with it.

It is likely that the procedures with price indices such as the CPI have been satisfactory enough over many years, so much so that perhaps any important modification would have been unwarranted. But this finding is related to factors of historical experience which are capable of unfavourable fluctuations. There is demonstration of this in some recent years. Abrupt events give abrupt characteristics to inflation

which destroy the possibility of an effective summary by any single
number. Out of regard to this, there is reason to have more ample
statistical reports which would communicate a knowledge of inflation
structure. Such structural information is essential for approaching
matters to do with income distribution, changes in the relative position
of different groups, taxation and inflation accounts in general.
Questions to do with purchasing power measurement are not at all new;
rather, they are among the oldest in economics. But there is a different
emphasis in the way they are imposed nowadays, requiring a different
response.

Professor Dahrendorf, in the remarks quoted in the Preface,
points out a general phenomenon, illustrated by the interest given to
differences of the effects of inflation on different consumer groups.
Thinking in terms of price indices is not the natural way to recognize
such differences. It should be established what is the actual extent of
these differences, and what is the effective and intelligible way of
stating them in detail and in a summary fashion by means of suitable
statistics. An example from early history shows most plainly what is
involved.

2. *Fleetwood's student*

"Since money is of no other use, than as it is the thing with which we purchase the necessities and conveniences of life, 'tis evident..." - this was a fleeting moment of practical concreteness and clarity, before the rise of index-number theory and doctrines of the "price-level". William Fleetwood, in 1707, calculated how much it would cost to live in a certain way in his day and four hundred years earlier. Since he was addressing the matter to a university student, he took as his example the life of a student, and its necessities (4 Hogsheads of Beer, 6 Yards of Cloth, 5 Quarters of Wheat, etc.). He found that "£5 in H.VI Days" would make a student "full as rich a man as he who has now £20." He might have taken any other representative type and instead of the figures (£5, £20) obtained some others, say (25, 50) for a Civil Servant. In fact, as in Canada, he could have sampled the population finding 16,000 examples of the way people live. Then the single point (5, 20) would appear as one in a cloud of 16,000. Taking the average point, the centre of gravity of the cloud, which in the rather sparse cloud formed by just these two points would be (15, 35), he would obtain

$$CPI = 35/15 = 2.3.$$

This is good luck for the Civil Servant and bad luck for the student. For, on issue of this number from H.M. Statistical Office in 1707, the one would receive an adjusted income of £58.3, that is an amount more than the £50 needed, and the other would be given not £20 but only £11.7 on which he could not live as accustomed.

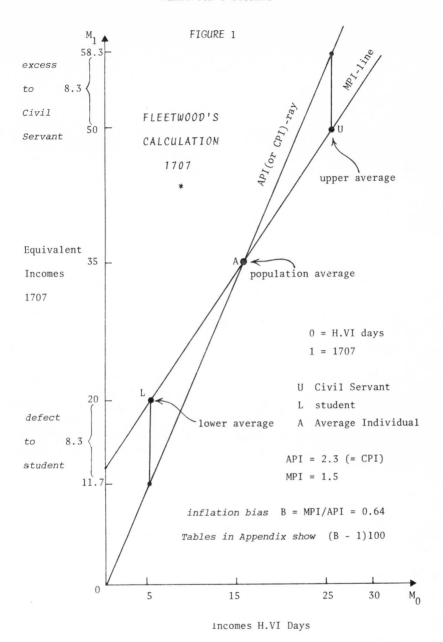

FIGURE 1

Incomes H.VI Days

Of course the bias could have been the other way round and in favour of the student. But there is no way of even taking notice of such bias, one way or the other, if it is a rule that just the CPI is to be used.

With reference to the Figure, the CPI is used to specify a homogeneous linear relation between equivalent incomes, represented by the ray through the point A. If the inflation adjustments determined from it are applied to all incomes, the total adjustment for the total of all incomes is correct, but the allocation of the total to the individual incomes is not. One broad aspect of this misallocation is that one half of the population, the upper or lower half (in the Figure it is the upper half) receives an excess, and the other half has a defect of equal amount. Any line through A will have the same merit as the CPI-ray as giving a relation between equivalent incomes which provides the correct total adjustment. But there is *just one* such line which moreover can make no dispute between the upper and lower halves since it divides the *total* between them correctly. This is the line which passes through U and L, whose slope defines the MPI. Though this line gives the correct allocation between the halves, it need not give the correct allocation between strata within the halves, except when the population consists in just two individuals, as in the chosen illustration which elaborates Fleetwood's calculation with one individual. This illustration can be taken further, by the method shown in Appendix I.

The average income £15 in H.VI days has been correctly adjusted to £35 in 1707. But the uniform proportion in which the adjustment is distributed to incomes is not correct. It would be better

to use the average price index or API (= CPI) 2.3 to determine the

average income

$$35 = 2.3 \times 15$$

for 1707 from that in H.VI days. Thus, in the Figure, 2.3 is the slope

of the ray through the overall average point A. Then instead of using

the usual proportionate, or homogeneous linear relation

$$M_1 = 2.3 \, M_0$$

for adjusting individual incomes, calculate the marginal price index or

MPI, 1.5, for adjusting deviations from the average, so as to form the

general linear relation

$$M_1 - 35 = 1.5(M_0 - 15).$$

In the Figure, 1.5 is the slope of the line joining the points U and L

which represent averages in the population where incomes are above and

below the median. For the student with $M_0 = 5$ this relation gives

$$M_1 = 35 + 1.5(5 - 15) = 20,$$

and for the Civil Servant with $M_0 = 25$ the result is $M_1 = 50$, as required.

The API and MPI ideas, which in an alternative terminology

are the inflation rate and incremental rate, for a group in the popula-

tion and a range of expenditure items, are discussed in the Appendix

together with illustration by calculations with Statistics Canada data.

The student and the Civil Servant here should be understood as average

representatives of two halves of the population, the division being by

income level. The shift from the API (or CPI)-ray to the MPI-line shown in the Figure corrects the bias which gives an excess of inflation adjustment to high incomes, and a corresponding defect to low incomes. The bias could well be opposite. The report *Prices and the Poor,* which is discussed in the next section, argues a bias unfavourable to low incomes in 1973. Our arithmetic with Statistics Canada data will confirm this, and quantify it. However it will be seen also that in other years, for instance 1967, the sense of the bias is reversed, though the degree is less (see, for instance, Table II).

The CPI (= API) is often understood to have use as an inflation adjustor of all money amounts, regardless of whether these be actual incomes or any other type of amount. In this it has the role of an *index of general purchasing power* of money. But just in the distinction between the API and MPI there is a refutation of the general possibility of having such an index which can meet criteria of fidelity in such a role. A much better candidate for a "general purchasing power" role is the MPI. But then the role has to be restricted. While the MPI alone does not specify adjustments to incomes it can, in an intelligible way which can be developed, specify adjustments of all money amounts which modify incomes and which, to allow for inflation, are to be adjusted to represent the same modification "in real terms".

A simple but most important step, taken already in the way Fleetwood's calculation has been reported and elaborated, and which occurs throughout this work, is the change from thinking in terms of simply a "price index" to thinking of *relations* between incomes with the same "purchasing power" or of points in the space where such a relation is represented. Then a price index is seen as just a homogeneous linear relation on this space, and, when there is need, it can be abandoned for a relation which is more suitable.

A document which is an eloquent representative of a particular dissatisfaction in having the CPI as the single arbiter in all matters to do with inflation is:

Prices and the Poor — A Report by the National Council of Welfare on the Low-Income Consumer in the Canadian Marketplace, 1974.

The phenomenon pointed out by Professor Dahrendorf is on the surface of this report.

A key statement in it has immediate correspondence with the idea of Fleetwood:

"The adequacy of an income depends upon the expenses that it must be adequate to meet. A greater number of dollars is no gain at all if it buys no more than the lesser number formerly did." (p.1)

More of what? — there is an ambiguity here, found also in Fleetwood.
It should be removed or there could be hazard of unprofitable talk
about "utility", such as followed Fleetwood. Instead it could be said:
a greater number of dollars is no gain if it cannot buy exactly what the
lesser number formerly did — that is the same bundle of goods. This is
really what is meant, or at least this is the meaning which shows in the
arithmetic of Fleetwood and of the CPI. Needless to say, if the greater
number of dollars can buy exactly what the lesser did formerly, together
with any saving, then it is a gain.

While Fleetwood's calculation dealt with the incomes of an
individual, taking into account "the expenses that it must be adequate
to meet" the CPI considers an entire community in the same fashion, as
if it were an individual. Fleetwood calculates incomes M_0, M_1 which, in
two periods, can purchase the same individual consumption. The "CPI"
for the individual is then M_1/M_0. But obviously it is important to know
both M_0 and M_1, and not just their ratio. With the CPI, in effect, there
is calculation of total community incomes T_0, T_1 which in two periods can
purchase the total community consumption as observed in some representative
period (with the calculations to be done here this is 1969). The CPI is
then T_1/T_0. (Or introducing averages $\overline{M}_0 = T_0/N$, $\overline{M}_1 = T_1/N$ it is, more
familiarly, $\overline{M}_1/\overline{M}_0$, though the total community has more reality than the
"average individual".) But the community consists in many individuals.
For any one individual an M_0, M_1 might have been calculated separately,
depending on the "expenses" of that particular individual. There is no
reason for M_1/M_0 for one individual to be the same as that for another, or

for the community. With $T_0 = \Sigma M_0$, $T_1 = \Sigma M_1$ and the M_1/M_0 varying, none needs coincide with T_1/T_0. Of course, should the M_1/M_0 all coincide with each other then they would coincide also with T_1/T_0. The validity of the CPI as a faithful representative of the inflation impact on all incomes depends on this special circumstance. The report *Prices and the Poor* compels attention to the unreality of such an assumption.

It is remarked "...a family with income of \$5,000 will not (be able to) buy one-third of the goods and services (that can be) bought by the family with a \$15,000 income". (Without losing the sense, and to isolate a part of it, we can omit the words in parentheses.) In other words, when income is tripled, or multiplied by any factor, purchases are not then all scaled correspondingly. On the contrary, the pattern of consumption, the proportions of things bought, changes even drastically. Some of the things enjoyed by the rich the poor cannot afford to buy at all. They have to concentrate their purchasing power on first necessities. Also the rich do not want to buy just so many times of everything the poor buy. On the contrary, they would rather have none of some things the poor must buy just in order to survive.

There are a number of other observations in *Prices and the Poor* which argue for the inadequacy of any uniform treatment of incomes such as that demonstrated in the uniform use of the CPI. Here the concern will be mainly with the aspect of the report going around this obvious but neglected variability of consumption patterns.

Certainly the uniformity issue about the CPI affects all incomes, favourably or unfavourably. But there is an understandable emphasis on its importance for low incomes. The point is made with the story of the man who drowned trying to wade across a river whose average depth, he had been assured, was a mere 18 inches. The crossing could no doubt have been made very routinely by a tall man, and no doubt this was a man of lesser height.

The argument is developed by pointing out that, according to 1969 data, families with less than $3,000 spend 27.9% of their income on food, while those with over $15,000 spend only 13.4%. Thus "any change in the price of food will have more than double the impact on those at the bottom of the income scale as it will have on those at the top". Or again, the "average" family, or the entire community, spends about 15% of income on housing, and about the same on transportation and travel. This is all that is taken notice of in constructing the CPI. However, the lowest-income fifth of the population spends three times as much on housing as on transportation and travel. But returning to food, in 1972 food prices began to rise more rapidly than other prices. The process continued through 1972 and then speeded up rapidly in 1973. "By December 1973 the food price index was 15.7 points ahead of the general index". Since the poor spend about 28% of their incomes on food while the population spends overall about 18%, the impact of inflation on the poor must be definitely greater than the average impact as given by the CPI.

Of course, the "food price index", which is the CPI computed for the population as if food was the only consumption, has the same defect already pointed out for the general CPI: it gives no recognition to the quite different diets enjoyed, or suffered, by rich and poor.

Also, food prices do not all change together, but rather the variations,

even for closely related foods, even for different grades of the same

type of food, can be quite different. No simple and satisfactory

correction of the CPI can be obtained for particular population groups

merely by readjusting the weights on aggregate indices, like the "food

price index", to correspond to their particular budgets. It is necessary

to go back to the original detailed, disaggregated data and start again.

In practice some form of aggregation is rather necessary. But in prin-

ciple, unless by chance this is organized on lines which maintain the

distinctions which are to be revealed, if indeed this is possible, these

distinctions will become masked to some degree in the results: they will

become blurred in a shift towards the average. Nevertheless the higher

the disaggregation, the better.

The year of *Prices and the Poor* is 1973; reference to

Table IV(b) shows an overall population inflation rate of 7.0 in that

year. But Table I(b) shows an inflation rate of 7.8 for the lowest octile,

where incomes are under $2,500, and 6.7 for the highest octile where

incomes are above $13,500. This strikingly confirms the qualitative

conclusion obtained for that year by the argument from the more rapid

rise of food prices and the greater share of income spent on food by the

poor. However, let it not be assumed that the bias of inflation is

always unfavourable to the poor. Table IV(d) shows an overall "inflation

bias index" of -0.5 in 1973, or a bias against low incomes of 0.5, which

is the highest absolute amount of bias for all the years considered.

However, the bias in 1971 is 0.4, against high incomes and in 1967 it is

0.3. Of course, in those years the inflation rate is lower than in 1973, and so the importance of any degree of bias is less.

It seems that inflation bias is increased when there are abrupt changes in the inflation rate. When the inflation rate has persisted around some particular level for a time, price changes could fall into harmony with it and this produces a uniformity, at least in medium term comparisons, if not in the short term. But a sudden change in the general or overall rate seems to be accompanied by non-uniformity. Abrupt economic events in the future could have this effect. We are reminded of the river of which only the average depth was known, and it would seem sensible to have a more detailed knowledge.

3. *What is a price index?*

Rather than search economic theory for the meaning of "price index" — this leads into a labyrinth where meanings often have become lost — it is simpler just to look at what a price index is in practice. All that is important for practice can then be gathered. But since the "index" language of economics has a long history and correspondingly complex associations, gathering strands of logic together with myth, it calls for a comment. The main point is the straightforwardness of the practical matter; it really lacks any of the mystery which is present with "index numbers".

No one speaks of "temperature index", at least not in Canada; it is enough to say "temperature". Whenever it is known what is being referred to the reference is simply to that thing. Even with "chill facto] there is a definition and we still know what we are talking about: the temperature which on a still day would produce the same rate of cooling on a standard body as the wind and temperature of the current day. Similarly with a price of a commodity we do not have an "index" of the price but just the price, that is, how much has to be paid — all this is certainly straightforward.   The "index" language comes in economics from complex compulsions to give numbers even when the meaning is not and perhaps cannot be known. When an unambiguous meaning for a number is not known it is an "index". The habit can inadvertently be carried into situations where there really is no occasion for it. This is the case with the CPI in its designation as a "price index". From the way the CPI is calculated its meaning is clear; just from its construction there is no compulsion to associate it with the "price index" idea and another name could tell more plainly what it is. From an important point of view, it becomes a price index especially from *the way it is used*.

The "price index" idea has one conspicuous meaning in the practical convention that any incomes M_0, M_1 in two periods which are to be determined as having the same purchasing power should correspond in a homogeneous linear relation $M_1 = P_{10}M_0$. Such a relation is specified by a single number P_{10}, its slope, and this slope is the "price index". There could be disagreement with this proposal as gathering essence of the idea. But there can be no controversy about meaning in the absence of a further distinction of meanings. Here there is settlement of a particular meaning, and a commitment to it. It might be objected that the choice is improperly narrow. Evidence for the judgement that it is not so but that it is everywhere at least implicit, even if not always fully explicit, in basic contexts and usages is offered by this book.

The ideas of "price index" and "price level" are certainly linked, and it can only be supposed that numbers offered in the role of the former are quantifications of the latter. It seems impossible to argue about this since no one knows the meaning of "price level" unless it is "price index". But there are many formulae for price indices. No matter, they are approximations to the "true" index — true no doubt because it truly represents the "price level". This closes a circle of meanings. To escape, a price index in practice is simply understood to be a number which has a certain use, and it is this use which qualifies the CPI as a price index. There can be question then about the extent to which this use is justified in the social context and how that extent should be described statistically. A suggestion about this is in the

Appendix. But the main propositions in this book are about the price

index as a term which belongs to theory rather than to practice. It is

important to see these two appearances of the term as separate. The

connection between them, which is simply a dedication to the homogeneous

linear relationship, is a matter of form and not of substance.

Two cardinal aspects of the typical price index of practice,

the CPI, are its construction and use which are essentially as follows:

(a) *Construction:* The CPI has reference to the total consumption of a

community for a range of commodities, as recorded by a sample survey in a

representative period, and compares estimates of the total cost of that

consumption at the prices in a base period and in any current period. The

percentage increase of that total cost from one period to another is the

community *inflation rate* from the one period to the other.

(b) *Use:* From one period to the other any income must increase by the

percentage given by the inflation rate, if it is to maintain the same

"purchasing power".

There are other uses, but this is the main one which has to be considered

and to which the others should be related.

The price index of practice is by most accounts identified

as a Laspeyres index. It is then put alongside another index which could

just as well be calculated were there the data for it, the Paasche index.

Then follows the "limits" proposition, which makes these indices theoretical

upper and lower units of the "true" index. Attributes of the Laspeyres

index in that theoretical context become transferred to the practical index,

and become part of the doctrine about its meaning. But about this there
can be complaints. To develop these, some ideas must be sorted out;
certainly if there is to be objection to the identification of the
practical index as a Laspeyres index, there has to be an understanding
about what these are.

As a matter of definition, $p_1 x / p_0 x$ is the *inflation factor*
for any bundle x between periods where the prices are p_0, p_1. It should
be asked if this automatically becomes a Laspeyres index merely by
setting $x = x_0$ where x_0 is any bundle of goods which, somehow, has the
date of the 0-period attached to it. Surely it does not, if the date of
the bundle, or the bundle itself, is an accident. Some stringencies
ought to be maintained in order to have a Laspeyres index, and not
something which merely has the same form.

A typical practical index like the CPI can have this form
in its original calculation. Thus it has a base year 0; but then there
is a *series* of current years 0, 1, 2, ..., not just *one* other, as
there is in the theoretical context where it is brought together with
the Paasche index (Ch. III). The CPI value for any current year i is

$$P_{i0} = p_i x_0 / p_0 x_0,$$

where x_0 is total community consumption in the base year. In other
words, it is the inflation factor between the base and current year for
community consumption in the base year. It is an inflation factor
determined in respect to the total community (or the "target" group) and,
incidentally, used as if it were the inflation factor for every individual in the group, which of course it is not, but that is a separate
matter. (See Appendix. Also note there has been confusion everywhere

in using the terms inflation factor and inflation rate.) It becomes

thought of as *the* inflation factor, from the base to any current year;

this then leads to thought of *the* inflation factor between any two

years i,j as being given by

$$P_{ij} = P_{j0}/P_{i0}$$

$$= p_j x_0/p_0 x_0 \ / \ p_i x_0/p_0 x_0$$

$$= p_j x_0/p_i x_0$$

In particular, the inflation *rate* across any one year is the inflation

factor between it and the previous year. Thus

$$p_1 x_0/p_0 x_0, \ p_2 x_0/p_1 x_0, \ \cdots$$

are the inflation rates for the first, second, ... years. But only the

first of these has the Laspeyres form. Generally, while the inflation

factors P_{i0} qualify at least in form as Laspeyres indices, none of the

equally well considered factors P_{ij} (j $\neq$ 0) do. Then, so to speak,

though any P_{i0} might seem to be born as a proper Laspeyres index, it has

sold its birthright as such when it is used to determine the other P_{ij}

and is put on the same footing as them.

What has been pointed out is that community consumption in

one particular year has been arbitrarily taken as the *standard* of

community consumption, and this has been made the basis for determining

inflation factors between any two years, in particular the inflation

rates across each year. Thus year 0 is, by arbitrary adoption, the

year of the standard, and then consumption x_0 in that year determines

the inflation factor $P_{ij} = p_j x_0/p_i x_0$ between any years i, j. While,

with the particular case j = 0, P_{i0} does have the Laspeyres form, this is not significant. The year of the standard is arbitrary, so there is only an accidental coincidence of the year j with that year. With a Laspeyres index the coincidence must be no accident.

Here is one manner of complaint about identification of a typical practical index as a Laspeyres index, going mainly around accidents about dates. Another manner involves the nature of the bundle x_0 as an aggregate. But first clear away all features on which the first complaint depended: suppose there are only two periods 0, 1 in view, and allow that coincidences of dates in the formula $P_{10} = p_1 x_0 / p_0 x_0$ are essential, so it has the form of a Laspeyres index in an essential way. Is this then a Laspeyres index? Historically, it could well be; this could be the arithmetic formula originally exploited by Laspeyres. From its form, it is one of the 126 (or by another count, 145, see Introd. Ch. III) formulae to be found in Irving Fisher's book. To make a distinction — though it is without any precise regard for history — let this be called the *original* Laspeyres index.

It has been argued that there is no good purpose, but a misleading intrusion, to even bring this formula in when giving account of methodology of the CPI and the inflation rates. An enlargement of that methodology is in the Appendix. The question now is whether, with any advantage, the original index can be identified with what will be called the *theoretical* Laspeyres index, that is the index which enters with the role of upper limit in the "limits" proposition (dealt with here in Chapter III). Doubts can be developed, on two independent scores: the nature of x_0 as an aggregate in the original index, and the presence of the Paasche index which is required with the theoretical index. The first of these by a mutual assistance of artifices can be put aside,

though it still deserves pursuit. The second is more resistant.

It should be appreciated that an important value of this

discussion — beside simply that it is compelled now — is to put restraint

on a ready reflex which brings all things which have a look of Laspeyres

indiscriminately together. Especially wanted is to break the celebrated

but spurious association between the practical index and the theoretical

index. This has already been done: the significant practical index is

$P_{ij} = p_j x_0 / p_i x_0$ and, except when accidentally i = 0, it does not even

have Laspeyres form. This brings about dissociation from both the original

index and the theoretical index, since the form is essential in both

these. Especially in view here is North American practice; practice in

the UK is somewhat different and a remark will be made about this

difference later.

But still, it is interesting to pursue any possible link

between the original and the theoretical indices. After all, the original

(single and not serial like the CPI) index could have standing as a

practical index; and in any case this is where the practical-theoretical

association probably began, and then became maintained by the illusion

that the modern North American year-to-year index is still a Laspeyres

index of any sort.

The first ground for reservation about the practical-theore-

tical association is that x_0 is an aggregate. The price-index of the

theory shown in Chapter III involves the hypothesis that demand is

governed by a utility order. That is, not only are wants, as expressed

by the hypothetical utility or preference order, fully deliberate, but

also there is perfectly precise programming with them. At least from
the standpoint of theory this is a bearable picture if the consumer is
a single individual — in fact, economists are accustomed to it. But
when the consumer is an entire community it is an absurd one — even
though theoreticians have made strong efforts to come to terms with
one definitely like it. How and on what basis is it possible for a
community to arrive at a preference order in their aggregate consumption
space? After all, each individual would consume only a bit of the
aggregate, and it may not even be clear what bit; and in the classical
picture the individuals are blind as "windowless monads" (Leibnitz),
they take no notice of each other, and so to each the community does not
even exist, let alone community preferences. Economic theory gives
training in such questions; but rather than face difficulties, suppose
they do not exist and that collective preferences for aggregate
consumption already make sense. Then there still remains a difficulty:
it is hard to entertain that precise aggregate consumption programming
with the collective preferences should be accomplished as a result of
every individual acting alone — free of any guidance from each other or
from a Great Conductor. Certainly it is extravagant to treat any
collection of individuals automatically as a single Gross Individual
having deliberate preferences for aggregate consumption and acting on
them very precisely. But at this point it should be noticed that something very much present has been left out: the homogeneity of utility,
which is an indispensable part of any price-index thinking. Possibly
this inescapable imposition also permits entry of a different point of
view which bypasses these obstacles.

Since $P_{10} = p_1 x_0 / p_0 x_0$ is unchanged when x_0 is replaced by any point on the ray through x_0, it is a function not so much of the point as of the ray. With any collection of consumptions, the aggregate and average lie on the same ray. Therefore it makes no difference to P_{10} whether x_0 is the aggregate or the average. Suppose all individuals were to be regarded as having the same utility, so their consumptions are different only because their incomes are different. With homogeneous utility, when prices are fixed the locus of consumption for all levels of income, or the expansion locus, is a ray. Then the consumption of all individuals in any period should lie on the same ray; and in reality they do not. The departure they have from being in the same ray can be regarded as due to "error". A statistical "estimate" can be made of the ray from which they have erred. This ray, which should be a kind of "average" of the rays through the individual consumptions, can be determined as the ray through the average consumption. In this way P_{10} with x_0 as average, which is the same with x_0 as aggregate, and as any point in the same ray, becomes regarded as determined for the ray which is the estimated locus of consumption for all individual consumers in period 0, and no longer as being simply for the aggregate. This dissolves the difficulty about the Laspeyres index being determined practically for an aggregate, while the theory applies to an individual. For now the aggregate index becomes identified statistically with the Laspeyres index for an individual, in fact every individual. Here also is a rationalization of the way the practical index, determined for the aggregate, is used indiscriminately for every individual.

The characteristic property of a ray is that if any points

lie on it then so does their sum, and so also does their average. It
gives basis for the "homogenization" of a group of consumers by taking
the ray through their average consumption as estimate of the locus on
which their consumptions should in principle all lie. From this flows
again the usual homogeneous treatment they receive from use of a price
index in practice. Also with this homogenization of individuals comes
the possibility of treating the group as just another individual,
governed by the same utility as they, whose income is the sum of their
incomes and who with it purchases the sum of their consumptions. In
other words, within the framework resulting from the homogenization,
the picture of the group behaving like an individual, having definite
wants and budgeting for them with precision, which has been claimed to
be unsuitable, comes with an appearance of validity.

A device has been found for connecting the index for an
aggregate with that for an individual, seeming to open a way for
propositions from theory to have some bearing on practice; but this is
what now has to be examined. Already it has been argued that the
familiar current practice is divorced from any significant theory
outside itself: it consists simply in determining inflation rates for
a standard bundle of goods. There is nothing further to add in that
connection. The concern now must be with the simpler situation
embodied in what has been called the original index, not serial but
involving just two periods 0, 1. It should be seen what price index
the theory shown in Chapter III has to offer there. As can be appreciated, that theory in earlier irresolute manifestations has been
without a complete control for its interpretations, but with loose ends

tied up it has become sterilized so as to be transparently without any immediate practical bearing.

The theory arbitrarily, from a tradition which could be regarded as an accident, concerns itself with just a pair of demands (x_0, p_0), (x_1, p_1). It then asks, or at least it should ask, if there exists a price index P_{10} compatible with these, and if there does then what are all its possible values. The answer is a formula for an interval, and this involves a pair of formulae which incidentally are the Paasche and Laspeyres formulae $\check{p}_{10}$, $\hat{P}_{10}$. If the interval is empty, which is when Paasche exceeds Laspeyres, which indeed could be the case, then there is no compatible price index at all. Then Laspeyres is not even admissable as a price index, and nor is any other number. This situation leaves a practical-theoretical dilemma: there is an absolute practical determination to construct a price index — after all, the Government, and the People, are waiting to hear what it is — while there is the absolute theoretical conclusion that one does not exist which is compatible with the data. No doubt the practical-theoretical economic statistician would be fired and replaced by one who has an undivided appreciation of his duties. In effect this has already been done: no one in normal practice bothers with theory, and quite rightly. Practical instinct has dispersed the clouds of theory, even the starry hosts of formulae, to settle on the one simple and sensible thing to do, which is closer to what Fleetwood did in 1707 than to anything else.

This argument could be prolonged: what if Paasche does not exceed Laspeyres, or what if Paasche is even not known? But the point is already amply put. The interests dictated by the social-economic

needs and statistical practicalities are different from those which arise
in the theoretical context.

From the standpoint of standard, or at least of North
American practice, Paasche and Laspeyres are not Paasche and Laspeyres;
they are inflation factors between two periods for two different
standard bundles of goods. Of course, there would be interest to know
what difference the change of standard makes to the inflation factor.
But there is no general reason why the change should produce an increase
or a decrease — there is no general inequality constraint between
"Paasche" and "Laspeyres".

The standard bundle of goods should correspond to a
prevailing pattern of living. It is determined by survey in a particular
year; but pattern changes with time, so as years pass it loses present
relevance. While in North America the standard bundle is based on a
large survey sample and is renewed every few years, for instance in
Canada it is based on a sample of about 16,000 households and was
renewed in 1961 and 1969, in the UK it is based on a small sample of
about 7,000, and is renewed every year. The inflation factor across
any span of years is then determined by compounding the inflation rates
obtained in each of the years. This is still more remote from the
Laspeyres index than anything in North America. It is more comparable
with the Divisia index — but no more than the North American is comparable
with Laspeyres. There is a strong merit in the UK practice. It is a
practical merit, not accountable within the usual theory, where
comparisons between times depend on hypothesis of a utility order which
is independent of time, though there can be some appreciation of it

by reference to that theory. A common complaint which applies
to the North American index is that, because the standard
bundle is fixed, when relative prices change it is not sensitive to
"substitution". It is the familiar argument: if tea has a price rise
relative to coffee, rather than buying still the original bundle, the
same utility would be obtained at less cost by sacrificing some tea
and buying more coffee, in other words the same standard of living
would become represented by a different bundle of goods, one cheaper
at current prices than the original. In *Prices and the Poor* (p.11) it is
pointed out that someone already buying only the cheapest food would
have no substitute to go to when food prices rise. Indeed, it is easy
to talk about "substitution" and to recognize its reality, but not easy
to give it explicit description and allowance. However, with UK
practice there is an implicit allowance, since the standard bundle is
undergoing continual revision from current statistical observations.

Substitution can be illustrated from utility theory, as is
familiar to every student. Demand analysts might then want to account
it econometrically on the basis of utility — taking the means for a
simple illustration as also the means for giving an actual account.
But changing as rapidly as relative prices is everything else in history
affecting living patterns. Utility analysis would be a manner of
attempting to identify a fixed structure underlying a surface of change.
However, there is no general reason, and no statistical experience
even suggesting its effectiveness for that. Rather, as soon as utility
is thought about as fixed, it has to be thought about as changing, and
if it is changing it cannot be observed — this is its *reductio ad absurdum*.

However UK practice is sensitive to "substitution" without venturing into absurdity.

A price index is directed to the relation between incomes in two periods which are to be regarded as being equivalent in purchasing power. It postulates a homogeneous linear relation, for which it gives the slope. Thus it involves a very special restriction on the relation. It is important to see this restriction, which from habit has become largely taken for granted, against the general background on which it is imposed. A recapitulation, which is built on and illustrated by calculations in the Appendix, is as follows.

Any two different years where the prices of commodities are different can be indicated by 0 and 1. Where a comparison is to be given which distinguishes one period as the *base period* for the comparison and the other as the *current period,* these will be 0 and 1 respectively. It is recognized that an income of M_0 held by some person in year 0 should have become an income of some M_1 in year 1 if that person's way of life is not to have been disturbed by the price change. An understanding which prevails for general purposes is that the income M_1 is to be related just to the income M_0. Next to this is the broader recognition which gives relevance also to the type of the consumer, besides just the income level. But putting this broader view aside, there is the standard view that the income adjustment over a period to offset the effect of a price change should depend just on the income. Then the agreed social "yardstick" for income adjustments will be a table showing various incomes in the first period and corresponding to them the equivalent incomes in the second period. This has the scheme

M_0	M_1
.	.
.	.
$4,000	$5,048
$5,000	$6,480
.	.
.	.

e.g. 0 = 1969

1 = 1974

The same information could be given in the form

M_0	M_1/M_0
.	.
.	.
$4,000	1.262
$5,000	1.296
.	.
.	.

There is the general possibility here of having a different ratio M_1/M_0 corresponding to each income M_0. A distinctive feature of standard practice is that M_1/M_0 is a fixed number, constructed in respect to the two years 0 and 1, which applies uniformly to all incomes M_0. In other words there is a simpler scheme

M_0	M_1/M_0
.	.
.	.
$4,000	1.270
$5,000	1.270
.	.
.	.

the numbers in the second column being all the same. Another way of presenting this scheme is to specify the fixed number P_{10} used to form the homogeneous linear relation

$$M_1 = P_{10}M_0$$

between equivalent incomes in the two periods. This number is the price index.

This could seem a laboured account of a matter which is simple and familiar from everyday experience with price indices and in particular

with the CPI. But the explicitness gives detachment from a simplicity
and familiarity which has been so thorough as to obliterate perception
of alternatives. It shows the price index as not an especially natural
approach to the matter and allows the view of others which are more
flexible.

The *unthinkability* of a true price index, as a practical
matter rather than a formal concept, and with that the reality of the
issues raised in *Prices and the Poor,* is obvious and has long had
appreciation. Enquiry then could be about the burial of this appreciation,
under a surface of simplistics in theory and rituals in practice which
support each other in denying it. The appreciation is very simple, but
the denial is vast and this has interest. There could be a not fully
accounted, but compelling reason for it. The phenomenon seems important
for features of it which appear in other contexts in economics. However,
with the price index, a compulsion comes from the broad social reference
it has together with the social requirement of simplicity. It is part of
a social ritual the agreeability of which is a historical variable.

Robert T. Michael (1975) gives this quotation:

"A perfectly exact measure of purchasing power is not only
unattainable, but even unthinkable. The same change of prices
affects the purchasing power of money to different persons in
different ways. For to him who can seldom afford to have meat,
a fall of one-fourth in the price of meat accompanied by a rise
of one-fourth in that of bread means a fall in the purchasing
power of money; his wages will not go so far as before. While
to his richer neighbour, who spends twice as much on meat as
on bread, the change acts the other way."

A. Marshall (1886)

I : THREE PROBLEMS

Introduction

This book deals with three mathematical problems each more
special than its predecessor. One purpose is just their formulation,
but also they are solved and various discussions go around the way this
is done.

It might seem from pure logic that a problem could stand
alone, like a monolith in empty space, but this is not the usual way
with problems. They belong to currents from which they cannot be separated, so if the current dries up perhaps they would disappear. These
three problems are in a particularly well-known voluminous but sickly
current: economic index numbers. In this there is a widespread practice,
and then there are theories which go around but which, it has been argued
here, have little to do with the practice, and there are myths. Corners
of the problems have broken the surface but they never would float into
full view, and to make them do that is an objective here. There should
be some appreciation also of the current which carries them, since otherwise they would have no sense.

Three well-known characters also are in that current like three
men in a boat. These are the price index formulae of Laspeyres, Paasche
and Fisher. With them is an amount of baggage, including a True Index,
an Ideal Index, a pair of "limits", a faulty Index Number Theorem, various
utility functions, including quadratics, a device called Revealed Preference, other related devices, and more. The problems at first show no
mention whatsoever of these characters, but when they are solved they
take on the appearance of a boat which carries all three together with

the baggage.

The familiar trio Laspeyres, Paasche and Fisher therefore are the chief characters. But others claim attention. In fact they also are familiar and in other settings have appeared as chief characters themselves. It is interesting how they act together, to make complication out of simple questions, which in the end have simple answers. The answers could seem to have been known all along, had the questions been known.

To boil the subject down to three problems and their solution would do injustice to its peculiar pathology. The problems and the methods used for dealing with them make a structure with some interest in itself to those with the inclination; for them it could stand as a small monolith in rather empty space, in fact a chip from a larger one which might have subsequent attention. This would leave out the broth from which the crystallization took place but what remains is at least straightforward. The original traditional subject, however, does not have such a regular character. A microanalysis of it is not possible within the limited space and intentions here, nor perhaps would it do service. On that side as in economics, a cryptic macroanalysis can be more brief and also cut better.

The main work here can be regarded as a repair done on a limited part of what is understood as the Theory of Index Numbers, the part where Laspeyres and Paasche enter, and then Fisher. It is not a minimal repair: there has been interest in the methods exceeding the need of the application. By these methods everything is capable of

being put more generally, but then more machinery must be brought in
and connection with the ancient lore becomes buried in the weight of
it.

The work therefore has different aspects. It is an exercise
in making definitions and formulating questions and propositions in terms
of them, within a framework made by ideas which are standard but are
capable of non-standard variations which show them better for what they
are. As such it is exercise in basic grammar of a part of economic
theory.

Another aspect is mathematical. The reference everywhere
here is to just a pair of demands, but statements have counterparts
for any finite number, so this is an introduction to a more general
mathematics. Here the proofs of propositions are simple and immediate,
while in the further theory, without adding to basic ideas, they are
comparatively long and elaborate. This theory for a finite collection
of demands, instead of for a demand function which is a particular kind
of infinite collection, makes a development in demand analysis called
Combinatorial Theory of Demand (Afriat (1976)). The book shows some
main features of that subject in a simple form. A striking product is
the equivalence of counterparts of the so-called Axioms of Revealed
Preference of Samuelson and Houthakker to the consistency of a system
of homogeneous linear inequalities, any solution of which permits the
construction of a finitely computable utility function which fits the
demand data. The integrability question which has a central place in
corresponding theory for demand functions evaporates in this finite
context and is replaced by a quite different pattern.

These are aspects of the work which, though not accidental by-products, are secondary to the declared purpose, which is to give a certain account of "the price index". Possibly there should be three main phases in a study of that idea: (i) everyday practices with "price indices", the statistical arithmetic and conventional uses, (ii) theory about the price index, which should give account of it as a theoretical concept, and is often supposed to have a bearing on (i), and (iii) the appearances in many economic theories of the term "price level", no doubt quantified by "price index". Here the main concern will be with (ii) for its own sake and also for impacts on (i). There will be no attention to (iii), though crystallization of the price index as a highly restrictive concept has a bearing there.

One type of discussion which is recognized as theory of index numbers is a branch of utility theory, and that will be a subject here. In the approach to be followed, questions are asked of the data and the formulae come afterwards in the answers. Next to that is an approach to index numbers associated especially with Irving Fisher, which can be distinguished from the utility theory though in many accounts they are not separated. In that approach, formulae are considered involving price-quantity data for two periods, in fact a very great variety of formulae, and there is no limit to their proliferation. In this maze of index formulae, which Fisher compared and classified in various ways, it is a puzzle to know which one is the "true index". It is believed that prices, though they be many, have a "level", and the "true index" is a ratio which compares levels in two periods. Thus

$$P_{rs} = P_s/P_r$$

is the price index with r, s as base and current periods, where P_r, P_s are the price-levels. In that case, for any three periods r, s, t necessarily

$$P_{rs}P_{st}P_{tr} = 1.$$

This is Fisher's Circularity Test. Consequences of it are

$$P_{rr} = 1$$

$$P_{rs}P_{sr} = 1$$

$$P_{rs}P_{st} = P_{rt}.$$

These also are "Tests", the first being the Identity Test, the second being Fisher's Reversal Test, and the third his Chain Test. If there is a formula for the "true index" it must satisfy these. The search made was disappointing, but Fisher had one which satisfies the Reversal Test and this is his "ideal index".

Since the Circularity Test, or the Chain Test which is its equivalent, is necessary and sufficient for any numbers P_{rs} to be the ratios of some numbers P_r, in particular of $P_r = P_{kr}$, for any fixed k, all that is involved here is what could be called the *Ratio Test*. Other conditions are claimed as "Tests" because they are consequences of this and they have no claim or meaning apart from it.

With $p_r \in \Omega_n$ as the prices in period r and $a \in \Omega^n$ some fixed bundle of goods, $P_{rs} = p_s a/p_r a$ is the *inflation rate* from period r to period s, *for the bundle of goods* a. These numbers satisfy the Ratio Test just from the way they are constructed. It could be wondered why this formula was not "ideal" for Fisher. Possibly it was too dull but, if he was looking for a more interesting one which meets the proper qualifications, it does not exist, as Eichhorn (1976) has shown. Unaccountably he arrived at a compromise which is neither proper nor dull.

1. The "Index Number Problem"

The so called "Index Number Problem" is an area of perplexity which comes from a use of terms whose meaning is not altogether known. From the insecure position that prices should have a "level", that level, whatever it should be, can be denoted P. Then P, which has thus been called into existence, joins the general furniture of economic discussion. It is available to become a part in some edifice, and even in many since there is no need to distinguish whether each appearance of P is really the same P or something entirely different. A problem arises only because there can still be pause to examine how P should be determined, granted that it exists. The tradition around the "Problem" shows no question of that existence and as far as possible the same restraint will be maintained here.

At the centre of the "Problem" is the "true index". This has reference to two periods, and is to be determined from prices and quantity data in just those periods. There is no criterion to admit an index as "true", and no definition of "index" except as a number which has a certain ritual in its production and use. An outstanding proposition is that the Laspeyres and Paasche indices are "limits", above and below. Then the "Index Number Theorem" is that one limit does not exceed the other. The affirmation is made regardless of the absence of any such general necessity. The geometric mean, which is the Fisher "ideal" index, is a superior "approximation" to either limit since it lies between them, and it is "ideal" because it satisfied Fisher's Reversal Test. Buscheguennce remarked Fisher's index is

"exact" if utility should be representable by a homogeneous quadratic.
The observation is still true though vacuous if no such representation
be possible, but it raises question about such possibility. Samuelson
pointed out the index problem involves an indeterminacy, liberating it
from a pursuit of the "true index" which, even if it existed and was
by chance encountered, could never be recognized.

This well-known lore makes the subject for study and interpretation. A conceptual definition of a price index and of the relevance of the data to its determination gives a position for calculating
the range of this recognized indeterminacy. The range could be empty -
thus denying the existence of an object with such indeterminacy - and
a question then is how to know by some test that it is not empty. The
"Index Number Theorem" bears on this test. It is not a theorem, but
it could be a trace of a theorem which emerged at some moment but part
of it, hypothesis or conclusion, got lost. Then a task is to recon-
struct the missing fragment. The Reconstructed Theorem shows the
usually considered inequality between the Laspeyres and Paasche indices as just the wanted test.

The entire matter has reference simply to a pair of
demands, giving prices and quantities of the goods. Various familiar
formulae apply to these and others can be added. For reference, various such features will be described in advance. But the genesis is to
be entirely in certain questions asked of the data, and anything which
is not in the surface of these must arise just out of their investigation. The immediate question (Problem I), which comes from the basic
concern with purchasing power decision to which the index is directed,

fails altogether to lead to the kind of statement wanted. Rather it contradicts the legitimacy of having a price index. This brings into relief that a special restriction is implicitly present in all thinking in terms of "price indices". This restriction will be stated in several different ways, one of which directly shows the use of a price index. It leads to a revised question (Problem II), and the theorems which are an answer to it give counterparts and enlargements of usual statements about the Laspeyres and Paasche indices. A further more restricted question (Problem III) elaborates Buscheguennce's remark about Fisher's index.

Though a logician could insist on a difference, the position at the end seems much the same as at the start. As in a very often quoted passage, "Everything is just as it was", and against "You'd generally get to somewhere else" is "Now, here, you see, it takes all the running you can do to keep in the same place. If you want to get somewhere else, you must run at least twice as fast as that." It is so also with the practice of index numbers since it still is at the point where it started with the calculation of William Fleetwood in 1707. The discussions since make a sustained current in economic literature, but still "Everything is just as it was."

Price indices are measurements without an ordinary object to measure. More, the object involved is a ritual with an embrace dictated from outside and unaffected by all the running you can do in the theory of index numbers. Only from change outside can come the recommended extra speed to get somewhere else. Such change is much present and recognized though, as already proposed, it is of no concern

here where attention is simply to the "price index" of the "Index
Number Problem". Even then the scope will be confined by a narrow
tradition in the problem, where always just two periods are involved.
But every aspect has a direct generalization involving any number of
periods simultaneously. The questions to be dealt with are capable
of alternative treatment, but there is influence from the particular
methods used, which lead immediately to generalizations and are part
of an approach which has other outcomes. To the suggestion that this
is like "using an atom bomb to boil a kettle" (words of an editor
delivering a rejection twenty years ago) an answer is that in any case
here is (or was) an interesting way to boil a kettle, and especially
so if otherwise that long-simmering kettle seems never quite to come
to a final boil.

2. *Formulae and tests*

There are two periods of consumption, the *base* and *current periods*.
0 and 1, and in these quantities x_0, $x_1 \in \Omega^n$ of goods are demanded at
prices p_0, $p_1 \in \Omega_n$. Then the incomes are

$$M_0 = p_0 x_0, \quad M_1 = p_1 x_1$$

and, provided M_0, $M_1 > 0$, budget vectors

$$u_0 = M_0^{-1} p_0, \quad u_1 = M_1^{-1} p_1$$

are determined, for which

$$u_0 x_0 = 1, \quad u_1 x_1 = 1.$$

The Laspeyres and Paasche "price indices" are given by

$$\hat{P}_{10} = p_1 x_0 / p_0 x_0 = u_1 x_0 M_1 / M_0$$

$$\check{P}_{10} = p_1 x_1 / p_0 x_1 = (1/u_0 x_1) M_1 / M_0$$

and the Fisher index is

$$\bar{P}_{10} = (p_1 x_0 p_1 x_1 / p_0 x_0 p_1 x_1)^{\frac{1}{2}}$$

$$= (u_1 x_0 / u_0 x_1)^{\frac{1}{2}} M_1 / M_0 .$$

Though it is not known what it is, the "True Index" is denoted P_{10}, and the
"method of limits" of Keynes (*A Treatise on Money*, Vol. I) gives the proposition

$$\check{P}_{10} \leqq P_{10} \leqq \hat{P}_{10} ,$$

and the "Index Number Theorem" is that

$$\check{P}_{10} \leqq \hat{P}_{10} ,$$

which is equivalent to the condition

$$p_0 x_1 p_1 x_0 \geqq p_0 x_0 p_1 x_1 ,$$

that is

$$(\dot{H}) \quad u_0 x_1 u_1 x_0 \geqq 1.$$

Samuelson's revealed preference argument applied to the demands (p_0, x_0),
(p_1, x_1) gives

$$p_0 x_1 \leqq p_0 x_0, \quad x_1 \neq x_0 \Rightarrow p_1 x_0 > p_1 x_1$$

or the same condition with 0, 1 interchanged. Another statement which is symmetrical between 0 and 1 is

$$p_0 x_1 \leqq p_0 x_0, \quad p_1 x_0 \leqq p_1 x_1 \Rightarrow x_0 = x_1,$$

that is,

$$(H^*) \quad u_0 x_1 \leqq 1, \quad u_1 x_0 \leqq 1 \Rightarrow x_0 = x_1.$$

If $x_0 = x_1$ then $u_0 x_1 = 1$, $u_1 x_0 = 1$, so H^* implies

$$(H) \quad u_0 x_1 \leqq 1, \quad u_1 x_0 \leqq 1 \Rightarrow u_0 x_1 = 1, \quad u_1 x_0 = 1$$

and this is implied also by $\dot{H}$. With the further condition

$$(\dot{H}^*) \quad u_0 x_1 u_1 x_0 > 1 \quad unless \quad \vec{x}_0 = \vec{x}_1,$$

$\vec{x}$ denoting the ray through x, there is the scheme

$$\dot{H}^* \quad \Rightarrow \quad H^*$$

$$\Downarrow \qquad \quad \Downarrow$$

$$\dot{H} \quad \Rightarrow \quad H$$

none of the converses being valid. This puts the "index number theorem" condition $\dot{H}$ and the more restricted modification of it $\dot{H}^*$ in relation with the Samuelson condition H^* and its relaxed modification H.

3. *Utility-cost*

A point of *satiation* of a utility order   R   is any   x   for which x < y   and   xRy   for some   y,   that is any bundle which is as good as a larger one.   Then   x < y => x$\overline{R}$y   asserts the absence of such points.

A utility order is complete if for any   x, y   either   xRy   or yRx,   that is   x$\overline{R}$y => yRx,   which can be stated $\overline{R}'$ ⊂ R.

For a general order   R   there is need to consider *critical cost functions*

$$\hat{\rho}(p, x) = \inf[py : yRx]$$

$$\check{\rho}(p, x) = \inf[py : x\overline{R}y].$$

These, as will be seen, coincide when   R   is complete and without satiation, but otherwise they have to be distinguished.

Since   xRx,   by reflexivity, it follows that

$$\hat{\rho}(p, x) \leqq px.$$

If   R   is without satiation, so   x$\overline{R}$y   for   y > x,   then

$$\check{\rho}(p, x) \leqq \inf[py : y > x] = px,$$

so also

$$\check{\rho}(p, x) \leqq px.$$

The significance of these functions for their application is shown in the following.

THEOREM   For any utility order   R   and any   p, x

(i)   *if   M > $\overset{\wedge}{\rho}$ then   yRx   for some   y   such that   py < M.*

(ii)   *if   M < $\overset{\vee}{\rho}$ then   y$\overline{R}$x   for all   y   such that   py $\leqq$ M,*

provided   R   is without satiation.

Since (i) is immediate from the definition of $\hat{\rho}$,   it remains to consider (ii).

Let $py \leq M < \check{\rho}$, so xRy by definition of $\check{\rho}$. Then there exists $z > y$ such that $px \leq \check{\rho}$, so xRz. But now if also yRx then, by transitivity, also yRz. But since $z > y$ this is impossible, by absence of satiation. Thus $y\bar{R}x$, and this proves (ii).

COROLLARY (i)   *For any utility order* R *and any* p, x

$$\hat{\rho} \leq \check{\rho} \quad if \quad R \quad is \ complete$$

$$\check{\rho} \leq \hat{\rho} \quad if \quad R \quad is \ without \ satiation.$$

The first part is immediate from the definitions. For the second, if $M < \check{\rho}$ then $py \leq M$ implies $y\bar{R}x$ for all y, by the Theorem. But this shows $M \leq \hat{\rho}$, by definition of $\hat{\rho}$. Thus for all M

$$M < \check{\rho} \implies M \leq \hat{\rho},$$

and from this follows $\check{\rho} \leq \hat{\rho}$.

COROLLARY (ii)   *If* R *is a complete utility order without satiation then* $\check{\rho} = \hat{\rho}$.

The Theorem shows, under the stated qualification, that for any x and p the cost at prices p of purchasing a bundle as good as x is at least $\check{\rho}$ and at most $\hat{\rho}$. The application the functions will have in determining cost bounds depends on this property, together with the following, which is immediate from the definitions. Let R_0, R_1 be any two utility orders, and let $\hat{\rho}_0$, $\hat{\rho}_1$ and $\check{\rho}_0$, $\check{\rho}_1$ be the corresponding critical cost functions. Then

$$R_0 \subset R_1 \implies \check{\rho}_0 \leq \check{\rho}_1, \quad \hat{\rho}_1 \leq \hat{\rho}_0.$$

Consequently:

COROLLARY (iii)   *For any utility orders* R_0, R_1 *without satiation*

$$R_0 \subset R_1 \implies \check{\rho}_0 \leq \check{\rho}_1 \leq \hat{\rho}_1 \leq \hat{\rho}_0.$$

and $\check{\rho}_1 = \hat{\rho}_1$ *if* R_1 *is complete.*

A *utility function* is any $\phi : \Omega^n \to \Omega$. It *represents* the utility

order   R   given by

$$xRy \equiv \phi(x) \geq \phi(y).$$

A *classical utility function* is semi-increasing, that is

$$x < y \Rightarrow \phi(x) < \phi(y)$$

and concave. These properties alone require the function to have a linear

support at every interior point of Ω^n, but a classical function is required

to have one also at any point on the boundary. For g to be the gradient of

a linear support, or a *support gradient,* at a point x the condition is

$$\phi(y) - \phi(x) \leq g(y - x) \quad \text{for all}\quad y.$$

Then, with ϕ semi-increasing, necessarily $g \geq 0$. A *classical utility*

relation is one which is representable by a classical function.

A *polyhedral* classical function is the especially simple type of

function determined by a finite set of supports. It has the form

$$\phi(x) = \min_{t} \phi_t(x)$$

where the ϕ_t are linear, with gradients $g_t \geq 0$. While for any utility

$\phi(x)$, the indirect utility function

$$\psi(u) = \max[\phi(y) : uy \leq 1]$$

is quasiconvex, and ϕ is recovered from ψ as

$$\phi(x) = \min[\psi(v) : vx \leq 1]$$

provided ϕ is quasiconcave, if ϕ is concave then ψ has the additional

property that $\psi(\rho^{-1}u)$ is a concave function of ρ, and so has a support

gradient $\lambda > 0$ at $\rho = 1$, for which

$$\psi(\rho^{-1}u) - \psi(u) \leq \lambda(\rho - 1),$$

giving

$$\left.\frac{d\psi(\rho^{-1}u)}{d\rho}\right|_{\rho=1} = \lambda$$

in case $\psi(\rho^{-1}u)$ is differentiable at $\rho = 1$. This λ, which here appears

directly as the marginal utility of income, also appears as the Lagrangian

multiplier in the condition

$$g \leq \lambda u, \quad gx = \lambda$$

for ϕ with support gradient g to be a maximum at x subject to the budget

constraint $ux \leq 1$, that is for x to be such that

$$\phi(x) = \psi(u), \quad ux \leq 1.$$

FIGURE 2

Utility-Cost

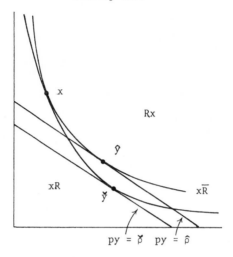

R is without satiation, so $\breve{\rho} \leqq \hat{\rho}$

and incomplete, allowing $\breve{\rho} < \hat{\rho}$

$\hat{y}$, $\breve{y}$ are in the closures of Rx, $x\bar{R}$ where

py attains lower limits $\hat{\rho}$, $\breve{\rho}$

R is typical of a revealed preference relation

with xR orthoconcave and

the consistency property xR $\cap$ Rx = {x}

and additionally Rx is orthoconvex

4. Cost-efficiency and efficacy

If a utility order R is given which is complete and without satiation so $\hat{\rho}$ and $\check{\rho}$ coincide in a single function ρ , then

$$M = \rho(p, x),$$

obtained from R, define the cost at prices p of maintaining a standard of living represented by a bundle x. Any income more than M is more than is necessary for the purpose, and any income less than M is less than sufficient (Section 3). This gives a concept of cost of living depending on a given utility relation R. The problem of the cost of living arises because usually the utility relation, by which it is intelligible as a concept and which is necessary for its determination, is not given. All that usually is given is a fragmentary scheme of data which has to be brought to bear in some way. An element of such data is a demand (x_t, p_t) , of quantities x_t at prices p_t , observed in some period of consumption t. The utility order R is to be constrained by having a relation to (x_t, p_t) . With several such demands being given at various times t, it is further constrained by being required to have that relation to each of them simultaneously. Then when R is constrained so is the value of $\rho(p, x)$ which depends on R. This shows a method by which the available demand data can be used if not to give a final determination of $\rho(p, x)$ then just to reduce its indeterminacy. But whatever might be proposed, it is sure than one way to maintain a standard of living represented by x, when the prices are p, is to have the income M = px adequate to purchase x itself. Practical procedure of cost of living assessment relies on just this. But the concern now is with theory in terms of utility, which, though it is consistent with everything in usual practice, adds nothing essential to it.

The needed relation between a utility order R and a demand (x, p) can have several versions. Most familiar is that given by the condition

$$(H^*) \quad py \leq px, \quad y \neq x \implies xRy, \quad y\bar{R}x.$$

If R is represented by a utility function ϕ, so

$$xRy \iff \phi(x) \geq \phi(y)$$

this becomes

$$py \leq px, \quad y \neq x \implies \phi(x) > \phi(y).$$

But R can be understood to be any order, just reflexive and transitive and not subject to any additional restrictions. The condition asserts that, according to R, x is the unique maximum among all bundles which, at the prices p, cost no more than x. Another way of stating this condition is

$$py \leq px \implies xRy, \quad yRx \implies py > px \quad \text{or} \quad y \neq x.$$

Then an apparent weakening of this condition, denoted H*, is H given by the conjunction of

$$(H') \quad py \leq px \implies xRy, \qquad (H'') \quad yRx \implies py \geq px.$$

The first part (H') here asserts that x is as good as any bundle which costs no more at the prices p. This is the principle of *cost-efficacy,* that the money spent on x has been spent effectively, since no better result is attainable with it at the same prices. Then (H'') is that any bundle which is as good as x costs at least as much, showing *cost-efficiency,* that it is impossible to reduce the cost and still obtain as good a result. These two conditions are generally independent. They represent the two equally basic criteria familiar in cost-benefit analysis. However, they become dependent if restrictions are imposed on R. Thus if yRx, y < x is impossible then H' => H'', and if R is complete, so $y\bar{R}x \implies xRy$, and the sets xR

are closed, then H" => H'. For instance if R is represented by a continuous increasing utility function then H' <=> H", and the same if the
function is just lower semi-continuous and semi-increasing.

The condition H = H(R; x, p) between a utility relation R and
demand (x, p) defines their *compatibility*, and the more strict H* defines
strict compatibility. They apply also to a utility function, through the
relation it represents.

There is always some utility compatible with a single demand
(x, p), $\phi(x) = px$ always being one example. But there does not always exist
a utility which is simultaneously compatible with two or more given demands.
To be able always to associate a utility with several demands simultaneously,
H must be relaxed in some way. This can be done by introducing a further
parameter e where $0 \le e \le 1$, representing a degree of cost-efficiency, and
replacing H by H(e) given by

$$H'(e) : py \le pxe => xRy, H"(e) : yRx => py \ge pxe.$$

This condition, defining *compatibility at a level of cost-efficiency* e, or
e-compatibility, is valid unconditionally if e = 0, and it coincides with
H if e = 1, that is H(1) ≡ H. Then with any given demands, even if e = 1
is impossible there will be the position to give e a small enough value to
assure the existence of a simultaneously e-compatible utility, because e = 0
is always one such value and such values have a readily determined upper limit
This more flexible method based on H(e) instead of H is suitable to the
present subject. But for simplicity and to maintain a direct relationship
with considered standard propositions   H will be adopted.

For R which is complete and non-satiated, so ρ̂, ρ̌ coincide and
can be denoted ρ, if also the sets xR are closed, so H" => H', making

$H \iff H'$, then a statement of compatibility H between R and a demand (x, p) is simply

$$\rho(p, x) = px.$$

But since generally $\rho(p, x) \leq px$, so $\rho(p, x) = epx$ where $0 \leq e \leq 1$, and the condition for e-compatibility $H(e)$ is

$$\rho(p, x) \geq epx,$$

there is always compatibility at the level $e = e(R; x, p)$ thus determined. With $u = px$ and $u = M^{-1}p$ this level is

$$e = \rho(u, x),$$

and the condition H requires $\rho(u, x) = 1$.

FIGURE 3

Demand-Utility Compatibility

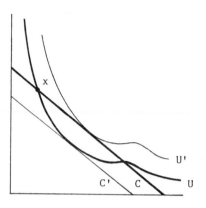

U   utility of x

U' utility of cost of x

C   cost of x

C' cost of utility of x

in any case

$$U' \geqq U, \qquad C' \leqq C$$

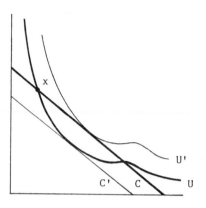

for compatibility between demand and utility

$$U' = U, \qquad C' = C$$

FIGURE 4

Partial Compatibility

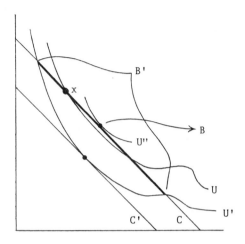

C   cost of x

C' part-cost of x

$$C' = eC, \qquad 0 \leq e \leq 1$$

U' utility of part-cost of x

U   utility of x,   U" utility of cost of x

partial compatibility: $U \geq U'$

e-compatibility, or compatibility at

a level of cost-efficiency e

compatibility $\equiv$ 1-compatibility

B' partial compatibility region, $x \in B'$

B   compatibility point

5. *The price index*

A price index is on the surface a number which is calculated by some formula and put to a certain use. Since the formulae for a price index are numerous - Fisher considered 126 of them, at least - and there is no conclusive way of choosing one from the other - Fisher showed it hardly mattered - it is impossible to discover a theoretical concept just from these formulae. Evidence for the theoretical concept involved therefore must come from the use.

A price index P_{10} is calculated with reference to two periods $0, 1$ in which the prices are different, and its use is to determine a relation

$$M_1 = P_{10}M_0$$

between any incomes M_0, M_1 in those periods which are to be accepted as having the same purchasing power. Inseparable from a price index is the presumption that the relation between equivalent incomes at different prices should be homogeneous linear. The entire meaning of a price index is that it should determine just such a relation by giving its slope. But the determination of equivalence between incomes has theoretical intelligibility with reference to utility. Thus, with a utility relation R and incomes M_0, M_1 at prices p_0, p_1 let x_0, x_1 be such that the demands (x_0, p_0), (x_1, p_1) are compatible with R and $p_0x_0 = M_0$, $p_1x_1 = M_1$, so these are bundles of goods the incomes might purchase at those prices. Then the condition for the purchasing power equivalence of the incomes M_0, M_1 at prices p_0, p_1 is that the bundles x_0, x_1 be indifferent in respect to R, that is x_0Rx_1, x_1Rx_0. This relation between M_0, M_1 obtained from any R and p_0, p_1 is a general monotonic increasing relation. That it be a homogeneous linear relation represents a special condition which has various equivalent statements, as follows.

(i)   In terms of preferences: xRy *implies* $xtRyt$ *for all* $t \geq 0$.

               That is, the utility order is conical.

(ii)   In terms of expansion loci: *compatibility with* R *for any*

(x_0, p_0) *is equivalent to that for* $(x_0 t, p_0)$ *for all* $t \geq 0$.

               That is, the expansion loci are conical.

(iii)   In terms of utility–cost: $\rho(p, x) = \theta(p)\phi(x)$ *where* θ, ϕ *are*

functions of p, x *alone.*

(iv)   In terms of purchasing power:

               any p_0, p_1 *determine* P_{10} *such that for all* (x_0, p_0), (x_1, p_1)

compatible with R *the indifference of* x_0, x_1 *with respect to* R *is equiv-*

alent to the relation $M_1/M_0 = P_{10}$ *where* $M_0 = p_0 x_0$, $M_1 = p_1 x_1$.

               There is still another form of statement in terms of a utility

function $\phi(x)$. Any budget constraint is described by $ux \leq 1$ for some

$u \in \Omega_n$. Then the budget constraint has a utility value, determined as the

maximum of utility attainable under it,

$$\psi(u) = \max[\phi(x) : ux \leq 1].$$

The utility of any budget constraint $px \leq M$ where $M > 0$ is the utility of

the constraint $ux \leq 1$ where $u = M^{-1}p$, that is $\psi(M^{-1}p)$. The condition

that any incomes M_0, M_1 have the same purchasing power at prices p_0, p_1

is now

$$\psi(M_0^{-1}p_0) = \psi(M_1^{-1}p_1).$$

This determines a correspondence between M_0, M_1 and the use of a price

index requires this correspondence to have the form $M_1/M_0 = P_{10}$ where P_{10}

is independent of M_0, M_1.

               When there is a price index P_{10} it must have the form

$$P_{10} = \theta(p_1)/\theta(p_0).$$

So to speak, it is a ratio P_1/P_0 of "price-levels"

$$P_0 = \theta(p_0), \quad P_1 = \theta(p_1).$$

The function θ is necessarily conical. So is the order R. Then if θ

is a function given to represent R which is not itself conical it can be

replaced by a function which is conical, and is equivalent in that it repre-

sents the same relation, and

$$X_0 = \theta(x_0), \quad X_1 = \theta(x_1)$$

are "quantity-levels"

$$P_0 X_0 = M_0, \quad P_1 X_1 = M_1.$$

Then $X_0 = X_1$ is equivalent to

$$M_0^{-1} P_0 = M_1^{-1} P_1.$$

That is

$$M_1/M_0 = P_{10}, \quad \text{where} \quad P_{10} = P_1/P_0.$$

This brings forward the link with the aspect of price index

thinking where prices have a "level", and a price index is a ratio of price

levels. Then follows the notion that the price index is to be grasped statis-

tically as some kind of average of individual price ratios - almost any kind

of average was Fisher's conclusion after studying together a great variety of

series based on different formulae. It also reveals the sense of Fisher's

Tests as tests that the set of price indices determined between pairs of peri-

ods should have consistency with their being a set of ratios. When there are

just two periods 0, 1 these tests reduce simply to

$$P_{01} = P_{10}^{-1}.$$

FIGURE 5

Income Purchasing Power

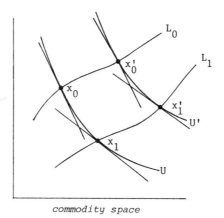

commodity space

p_0, p_1 any prices; L_0, L_1 corresponding expansion loci
U a utility level; x_0, x_1 bundles where U cuts L_0, L_1

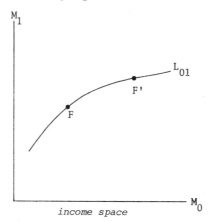

income space

L_{01} purchasing power relation, holding between incomes
M_0, M_1 having the same purchasing power at prices p_0, p_1;
it is described by points $F = (M_0, M_1)$ whose coordinates
$M_0 = p_0 x_0$, $M_1 = p_1 x_1$ are incomes purchasing the same utility U

FIGURE 6

Purchasing Power and the Price Index

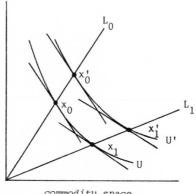

commodity space

p_0, p_1 any prices; L_0, L_1 corresponding expansion rays

U a utility level; x_0, x_1 bundles where U cuts L_0, L_1

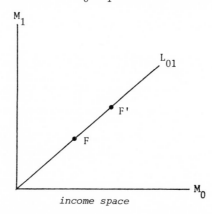

income space

L_{01} purchasing power relation, proportion $M_0 : M_1$ fixed

$M_1 = P_{10}M_0$ where P_{10} is the price-index

determined from one price position to the other

6. *Problems*

The definitions which have been made permit the following formulations.

PROBLEM I   *To establish a test for the existence of a utility order*
R *with which the given demands* (x_0, p_0), (x_1, p_1) *are simultaneously*
compatible and then to determine the possible values of the cost $\rho(p_1, x_0)$
at the prices p_1 *of maintaining the standard of living represented by*
the bundle of goods x_0, *determined in respect to all such orders.*

Instead of $\rho(p_1, x_0)$ in this problem there is no reason not to consider $\rho(p_s, x_t)$ where s, t are periods different from the periods 0, 1 of the demand observations, or $\rho(p, x)$ for quite arbitrary p, x and for demand observations taken from a collection of any number of periods. But the usual custom is to consider indices between two periods based on the data from just those periods.

The method with this problem will be to find bounds on $\rho(p_1, x_0)$ without any additional restriction on R, and then, as a subsidiary problem, to show that any point in the interval determined by these bounds is attained for some classical polyhedral R. This shows that the bounds are in fact limits, and also that the values exhaust the interval between them.

It also shows that the subsidiary problem gives no different result from the main problem. The significance of this is that the special properties for a utility function which are usually assumed and on which familiarly so much emphasis is made are without necessity or importance. For at first here no special properties at all are required for R, and then all properties usually considered and more are imposed, *but they make no difference,* neither to the consistency test nor to the range of values determined.

This basic first problem leads to an unfamiliar result without intelligibility in terms of a price index. It is the problem actually presented by Alan Brown in the lecture of 1953 mentioned in the Preface. Recognition of the price index as entirely a homogeneous concept leads to a reformulation.

PROBLEM II   *To establish a test for the existence of a homogeneous utility order which is compatible with the given demands. In respect to any such order* R, *the cost* M_1 *at prices* p_1 *of attaining the standard of living obtained by any income* M_0 *at prices* p_0 *has a fixed ratio* P_{10} *to* M_0, *defining the price index with* p_0, p_1 *as base and current prices, and all possible values of this index are to be determined.*

The test obtained, which is, as it should be, more restrictive than that obtained for Problem I (see Chapter I, Section 2), is the often considered "theorem" that the Paasche index should not exceed that of Laspeyres. Then the required set of values is the closed interval, lying within the formerly obtained interval, with these indices as limits.

Fisher's "ideal" index lies between these limits, and Buscheguennce's remark about its connection with quadratics brings into view the following still more restricted problem.

PROBLEM III   *To establish a test for the existence of a homogeneous quadratic utility with which the given demands are simultaneously compatible and then to determine all possible values of the price index in respect to such utilities.*

Investigation of this problem, which could be a first response to Buscheguennce's remark, leads to the conclusion that the problem should be modified. Instead of asking for a compatible homogeneous quadratic utility, the existence of which is awkward, it is better to ask for a

compatible homogeneous utility which has quadratic representation near

x_0, x_1. Then the test is simple and, surprisingly, it is identical with

that found for Problem II.

The automatic existence of a compatible homogeneous locally

quadratic utility whenever there exists a compatible homogeneous utility

suggests a tolerance which will leave a general indeterminacy as found

in Problems I and II, except just that the indeterminacy would be dimin-

ished still further by the additional quadratic restriction. This surmise

could seem to be reinforced by there being an infinite variety of locally

compatible quadratics, if there are any, assuming $n > 2$. In spite of

all this, the indeterminacy is removed totally, without defect or excess,

leaving a point determination which moreover is identical with the point

provided by Fisher's index.

If homogeneity is abandoned, while retaining the quadratic

requirement, simultaneous compatibility is possible in positive measure

just with two further demands, but nevertheless indeterminacy is restored

(Afriat 1956 and 1961, in Shubik 1967).

II : THE GENERAL PROBLEM OF LIMITS

Introduction

The distinction made between exchange-value and use-value for goods produces the idea that money, or — what is more specific and intelligible — any income, has a *purchasing power* which is variable depending on prices. The distinction is recognized, but at the same time there is need to avoid the awkwardness of maintaining it fully. The need must be understood, because otherwise there can bewilderment at consequences of it. One of these is the leap to the nebulous notion of the general purchasing power of money, or its reciprocal which, no doubt, is the price level. Keynes, who made much of the price level, found it unsuitable and offered retreat to a more accommodating idea which allowed a "plurality" of purchasing powers (*A Treatise on Money*, Vol. I); but also this is nebulous, it being simply a relaxation of an already nebulous idea. A different and also familiar perplexity with the distinction is in general equilibrium and welfare theory. There the distinction is between the exchange-value of output of the economy at equilibrium prices and the use-value in the .sense of collective welfare obtained. Under usual assumptions the former is indeed maximum for output at equilibrium, but in fact this is not recognized, and from doctrine it is the latter which should be maximum. But the latter is only a phrase without an identified meaning, though it can gather the appearance of this from confusion with the former — wizardry with the differential calculus produces just this illusion. In consequence equilibrium prices do not measure merely themselves but are proportional to "marginal product"; they become distinguished not just as equilibrium prices but as "efficiency prices" which lead the economy to maximum "welfare". A formidable structure has been built on circularities.

The market has value, even many values, in a sense which relates to its function and is alien from anything to do with magnitude. In theory, competition is enough to govern the market; so if, for instance, the single unswerving objective is elimination of dependence on any other form of government then it is indeed optimal, since such dependence is, at least in the model, completely eliminated. But here is quite another sense of value, in an unfortunate collision with others, and out of the wreckage of distinctions around it arises the mythical doctrine of maximality.

This digression, though it is important, is rather distant from the present subject. To be considered here is the distinction between the exchange-value of an income, stated by so-many $$, and the use-value which derives from what is done with it. The way this is developed depends on how the use-value is stated.

Consider a period 0 when prices are $p_0 \in \Omega_n$, and an income M_0 is spent on consumption of a bundle of goods $x_0 \in \Omega^n$. Income is understood to coincide with expenditure on the goods, equal to their cost at the prevailing prices, so

$$M_0 = p_0 x_0.$$

This limitation of what is meant by income fits the usual terminology in demand analysis, but it does not agree with income in any ordinary sense, about which there can be no neat theory of "purchasing power". Keynes remarks: "The importance of money essentially flows from its being a link between the present and the future." Dynamic involvements of income gathered in this remark entirely escape present considerations.

With Fleetwood (p. 12) the use-value of income M_0 in period

0 when the prices are p_0 would be simply the bundle of goods x_0. Then

for an income M_1 to have the same use-value, or purchasing power, in

period 1 when the prices are p_1, the condition is simply

$$M_1 = p_1 x_0.$$

This has validity when there is steadfast adherence to living-style, no

entertainment of "substitutes", and all that is wanted is to go on living

as before.   In this case there would be no buying of more coffee just

because there is a rise in the price of tea; in brief, an easily account-

able un-neoclassical condition of dignity prevails. But this is too

simple and there is not much to say about it. Instead now, each bundle

of goods is treated not as distinct individual use-value but as serving

a general usefulness, in a use-system which is fixed and independent of

time. But demand is history; there can be comment about it, on patterns

present and forces which have effect, but no complete mechanical account.

A utility ordering is supposed to persist through time, or be indepen-

dent of it — while it determines historical events, the demands which

take place in time. The pretence cannot be serious! An alternative

position is that a utility ordering prevails in any moment of time, to

determine demand in that moment, but it is changing with the time. But

all that is observable in any moment is simply the demand. It can be

said there is a utility ordering which determines the demand, a differ-

ent one in every moment. But this means nothing, no refutation is

possible, in other words there is no content to refute. Then certainly

the assertion can be upheld — it does not matter since it makes no

difference.

The utility hypothesis as a model of demand behaviour is just

a model, to be played with — as it has been, extravagantly. But in the
question of income purchasing power it does not have intention as a
behaviour model; rather, it provides a basis for intelligibility of the
question. It gives terms in which the question could be answered.
Because the question involves the hypothesis just in its being understood, any dissatisfaction with the hypothesis must be redirected towards
the question. However, the question itself escapes effective judgement
about being sensible or not, because it is already imposed from practicalities in social-economic experience: prices change, and then any income
must change if it is to maintain the same purchasing power — it is wanted
to know how much it should change. A similar question is with political
decisions: there are many candidates and one must be chosen — which one?
There is no single formula which tells how this must be settled; it is a
matter of design with many possibilities. The same holds with the purchasing power question. Practice has fixed an approach, but theory would
find this too simple for comment and takes up another — one quite familiar, an old help in the flight from disquieting unaccountabilities of
history into the illusion of permanent mechanism — utility theory.

A postulate of utility theory is that consumption bundles are
not distinct ends in themselves, each representative of a pattern of
living, but instead there is a further end, in the general service of
which they are all just alternative inputs. They are ranked together
according to the extent in which they can serve it. In other words, there
is an order R in the commodity space, that is a reflexive, transitive
binary relation, where xRy signifies the bundle x is as good, or useful,
for the purpose as the bundle y. The order R is fixed, independent of

time or anything else.   There is one non-committal element in this thinking:
the utility order R *is not specified.*

Suppose an order R is specified.   Let x be any bundle of goods
and p any price, and assume

$$\rho(p,x) = \min[py : yRx]$$

exists, as it must if Rx is closed and p > 0.   For any bundle y such that
yRx, an expenditure of money py suffices to buy consumption of at least the
standard of x, since it will buy y which is as good as x.   The cost of an
objective being the minimum expenditure adequate for attaining it, $\rho(p,x)$
is the cost at prices p for attaining the standard of consumption of x.
Necessarily

$$\rho(p,x) \leq px$$

since R is reflexive; that is, the cost of attaining the standard of x does
not exceed the cost of x itself.   In ignorance of R, there is nothing more
that can be said about ρ.   But should a constraint be put on R, there will
be a consequent constraint on ρ since it depends not only on p and x but
also on R.

When orders R are considered which must satisfy certain con-
straints, there arises the question whether any such orders exist.   A test
has to be found, and discovering this is the first problem which will be
considered.   The test is shown in several different but equivalent forms.
These serve the next considered problem, which is to determine all possible
values of ρ corresponding to all possible orders R which satisfy the con-
straints.   While $\rho = \rho(p,x)$ could well be considered for any p and x,
custom brings attention especially to $\rho_{10} = \rho(p_1, x_0)$.

The data on the consumer consists in the demands (x_t, p_t)

(t = 0, 1). This is all the data that are available, and if the order R
which is to apply to the consumer is to be restricted by relation to the
consumer, it can only be by relation to those demands. Then there is no
obvious alternative but to require that the consumer appear to be governed
by the order R in making those demands. For in the thought about the
order R is the presumption that the calculations based on it *will* govern
the consumer; and there is no available basis for supposing the consumer
should be governed by any order R except that it appears from observations
that the consumer has *already* been governed by R. In the absence of a
counterproposal there is only this to follow.

To formulate the questions which will be dealt with, it remains
to account the relation H applying between any order R and any demand
(x, p). This expresses the idea of the order governing the demand, or
generating it, or that the order and the demand together are *compatible*.
Then *consistency* of any demands is defined by the existence of an order with
which they are simultaneously compatible.

It is a premise in utility theory that a bundle of goods is not
an irreplaceable individual object bought just for its own sake, but that
the objective is its utility, which can be obtained also from many substitutes.
The money px spent in the demand (x, p) has then to be viewed not as
merely buying x but as buying the utility of x. While px is the cost of
x, at prices p, $\rho(p,x)$ is the cost of the utility of x, necessarily at
most px. If the consumer, in buying x, is truly buying just the utility of
x at its cost, the money px spent on x must coincide with the utility-cost
$\rho(p,x)$; that is, $\rho(p,x) = px$. An equivalent statement is that any bundle of
goods y which has as much utility as x would cost at least as much, that is,

(H")   yRx => py $\geq$ px.

By this condition H", the order R is such as to represent the demand

(x,p) as *cost-efficient*, meaning it is impossible to achieve the same

objective at a lesser cost.

But this condition, which asks that a given use-value be

obtained with minimum sacrifice of exchange-value, is only part of the

matter. It is the part compelled in order to give effect to the idea of

cost-of-living. But also present is the idea of the *purchasing power of*

incomes. While cost for a given gain in an objective, if it is to be

unambiguous, can only mean the minimum possible cost for attaining it,

similarly the gain from a given expenditure can only mean the maximum

possible gain obtainable by means of it. With Fleetwood (p.6) "...

money is of no other use, than as it is the thing with which we purchase

the necessities and conveniences of life ...". Here money instead

purchases utility. Then the purchasing power of an income, or its

use-value, is the highest level of utility attainable with it.

There can be no comparison of the purchasing power of

incomes without presumption that incomes realize their purchasing power.

Accordingly, with a demand (x,p), it is required that no bundle better

than x could have been bought with the same amount of money px. What

is the same, x is as good as any bundle of goods y which costs no more,

that is

(H')   py $\leq$ px => xRy

This condition H' shows the order R as representing the demand (x,p) as

cost-effective, meaning that for the same cost it is impossible to

achieve a superior objective.

The conjunction H of the conditions H' and H" defines the relation of *compatibility* between an order R and a demand (x,p). Consumers' demands (x_t, p_t) at times t = 0,1 are given, and any order R is considered with which they are simultaneously compatible. This makes the consumer represented not only as fully deliberate and constant about wants, described by the relation R fixed through time, but also as a completely precise programmer, at least on the occasions t = 0,1 when observed. In purchasing the bundle x_t at the prices p_t (t = 0,1) no bundle exists which is as good and costs less. Also, it is impossible with the money $p_t x_t$ spent, to buy a better bundle than x_t. The relation R is constrained simply by the requirement that it give this picture of the consumer as such a completely informed, deliberate, constant and precise individual.

For correspondence with experience, this picture is remote. But, fortunately, such correspondence is not here an issue. Rather, the picture serves to give a particular theoretical intelligibility to income "purchasing power" and "cost-of-living". Then it gives rise to formal questions which, being purely formal, can be pursued separately and in disregard of original merit. Then they acquire another merit just in the pursuit — if the enormous attention given to utility theory is witness.

1. *Consistency of demands*

Let (x_t, p_t) $(t = 0, 1)$ be two given demands, associated with two periods $t = 0, 1$. They are associated with incomes $M_t = p_t x_t$, assumed positive, and then budget vectors $u_t = M_t^{-1} p_t$, for which $u_t x_t = 1$. Then between them there are *cross-coefficients*

$$D_{st} = u_s x_t - 1 \quad (s, t = 0, 1),$$

for which $D_{tt} = 0$.

Let $H_t(R)$ assert the *compatibility* of demand t with a utility order R, this being the conjunction of conditions

$$H'_t(R) \equiv u_t x \leqq 1 \Rightarrow x_t R x$$

$$H''_t(R) \equiv x R x_t \Rightarrow u_t x \geqq 1,$$

expressing *cost-efficiency* and *efficacy*. The simultaneous compatibility of the two demands with R is the conjunction $H(R)$ of $H_t(R)$ for $t = 0, 1$, and the assertion H of this for some R gives their *consistency*.

Consider also the condition

$$K \equiv u_0 x_1 \leqq 1, \quad u_1 x_0 \leqq 1 \Rightarrow u_0 x_1 = u_1 x_0 = 1.$$

This just excludes the possibility

$$u_0 x_1 \leqq 1, \quad u_1 x_0 < 1$$

and the same with $0, 1$ interchanged.

THEOREM 1.1 $H \Rightarrow K$.

Suppose $H(R)$. Then, from $H'_0(R)$,

$$u_0 x_1 \leqq 1 \Rightarrow x_0 R x_1$$

and from $H''_1(R)$,

$$u_1 x_0 < 1 \Rightarrow x_0 \overline{R} x_1,$$

showing the required conclusion.

Another statement of K is that

$$D_{01} \leq 0, \quad D_{10} \leq 0 \Rightarrow D_{01} = 0, \quad D_{01} = 0$$

or that

$$(D_{01}, D_{10}) \leq 0$$

is excluded.

Any numbers $\lambda = (\lambda_0, \lambda_1)$ are a *multiplier solution* if they satisfy the condition

$$L(\lambda) \equiv \lambda_0, \lambda_1 > 0, \quad \lambda_0 D_{01} + \lambda_1 D_{10} \geq 0.$$

The assertion L of the existence of such numbers defines *multiplier consistency* of the demands.

THEOREM 1.2 $K \iff L$.

Since

$$(D_{01}, D_{10}) \leq 0, \quad \lambda_0, \lambda_1 > 0$$

implies

$$\lambda_0 D_{01} + \lambda_1 D_{10} < 0,$$

it follows that $L \Rightarrow K$.

To prove the converse, suppose K. Then either both D_{01}, D_{10} are zero or at least one, say D_{10}, is positive. In the former case L is verified, since $L(\lambda_0, \lambda_1)$ holds for all $\lambda_0, \lambda_1 > 0$. In the latter case it holds with $\lambda_0 = 1$ and $\lambda_1 > D_{01} D_{10}^{-1}$, so again L is verified, and the theorem is proved.

Any numbers $\lambda = (\lambda_0, \lambda_1)$, $\phi = (\phi_0, \phi_1)$ are a *multiplier-level solution* if they satisfy the condition

$$S(\lambda, \phi) \equiv \lambda_0, \lambda_1 > 0, \quad \lambda_0 D_{01} \geq \phi_1 - \phi_0, \quad \lambda_1 D_{10} \geq \phi_0 - \phi_1.$$

The assertion S of the existence of such numbers defines *multiplier-level consistency*. Also for any λ let $S(\lambda)$ assert the existence of ϕ such that $S(\lambda, \phi)$.

THEOREM 1.3 $L(\lambda)$ <=> $S(\lambda)$.

Since

$$\lambda_0 D_{01} \geqq \phi_1 - \phi_0, \quad \lambda_1 D_{10} \geqq \phi_0 - \phi_1,$$

by addition, imply $\lambda_0 D_{01} + \lambda_1 D_{10} \geqq 0$, it appears that $S(\lambda) \Rightarrow L(\lambda)$.

For the converse, $L(\lambda)$ implies

$$\lambda_0 D_{01} \geqq -\lambda_1 D_{10},$$

and hence the existence of ϕ_1 such that

$$\lambda_0 D_{01} \geqq \phi_1 \geqq -\lambda_1 D_{10}.$$

Then $S(\lambda, \phi)$ is verified with $\phi_0 = 0$.

COROLLARY   L   <=>   S.

For any given λ, ϕ introduce functions

$$\phi_0(x) = \phi_0 + \lambda_0(u_0 x - 1), \quad \phi_1(x) = \phi_1 + \lambda_1(u_1 x - 1)$$

and

$$\phi(x) = \min[\phi_0(x), \quad \phi_1(x)].$$

Let $C(\lambda, \phi)$ assert $H(R)$ where R is the utility order represented

by $\phi(x)$, and let C assert this for some λ, ϕ. Thus immediately

$$C \Rightarrow H.$$

THEOREM 1.4 $S(\lambda, \phi) \Rightarrow C(\lambda, \phi)$.

Since

$$\phi_0(x_0) = \phi_0, \quad \phi_1(x_0) = \phi_1 - \lambda_1 D_{10}$$

so

$$\phi(x_0) = \min[\phi_0, \quad \phi_1 + \lambda_1 D_{10}]$$

it follows that

$$\phi(x_0) = \phi_0(x_0)   \text{<=>}   \lambda_1 D_{10} \geqq \phi_1 - \phi_0.$$

Also

$$u_0 x < 1 \Rightarrow \phi_0(x) < \phi_0(x_0)   \text{<=>}   \lambda_0 > 0.$$

Since in any case

$$\phi(x) \leq \phi_0(x)$$

it now follows that if

$$\lambda_0 > 0, \quad \lambda_1 D_{10} \geq \phi_1 - \phi_0$$

then

$$u_0 x < 1 \Rightarrow \phi(x) < \phi(x_0),$$

and similarly with $0, 1$ interchanged. This shows that

$$S(\lambda, \phi) \Rightarrow C(\lambda, \phi).$$

To consider the converse, suppose $C(\lambda, \phi)$, so

$$u_0 x < 1 \Rightarrow \phi(x) < \phi(x_0).$$

Since $\phi(x)$ is concave, with a support gradient g_0 at x_0, this implies

$$g_0 \leq \mu u_0, \quad g_0 x_0 = \mu, \quad \mu > 0$$

for some μ. But either $g_0 = \lambda_0 u_0$ or $g_0 = \lambda_1 u_1$. In the second case $\mu = \lambda_1 u_1 x_0$, so $\mu > 0$ requires $\lambda_1 > 0$, and then $u_1 \leq u_1 x_0 u_0$. With $x_0 > 0$ this implies $u_1 = u_1 x_0 u_0$, that is, prices are proportional. Thus positive quantities and exclusion of proportional prices requires $g_0 = \lambda_0 u_0$, and then $\phi(x_0) = \phi_0(x_0)$, that is $\lambda_1 D_{10} \geq \phi_1 - \phi_0$. In this case $\mu = \lambda_0$, so $\lambda_0 > 0$. This shows the converse is valid at least under the qualification that all quantities be positive and prices in the two periods be not proportional.

THEOREM 1.5 $H \Leftrightarrow K \Leftrightarrow L \Leftrightarrow S \Leftrightarrow C.$

This follows from the foregoing theorems together with $C \Rightarrow H$.

For a classical utility function $\phi(x)$ with any point $x \in \Omega^n$ there exists $g \in \Omega_n$, a support gradient of the function at that point, such that

$$\phi(y) - \phi(x) \leqq g(y - x).$$

Then, given $ux = 1$, the compatibility condition

$$uy < 1 \Rightarrow \phi(y) < \phi(x)$$

is equivalent to

$$g \leq \lambda u, \quad gx = \lambda, \quad \lambda > 0.$$

Thus the particular function $\phi(x)$ constructed under the condition $S(\lambda, \phi)$ is classical. A support gradient g at any x is generally given by

$$g = \lambda_t u_t \quad \text{if} \quad \phi_t(x) \leq \phi_s(x) \quad (s, t = 0, 1).$$

But since, under the condition $S(\lambda, \phi)$,

$$\phi_t(x_t) = \phi_t \leq \phi_s + \lambda_s D_{st} = \phi_s(x_t)$$

it follows then that

$$g_t = \lambda_t u_t$$

is a support gradient at x_t.

With the indirect utility function, of any utility function ϕ, given by

$$\psi(u) = \max\lceil \phi(y) : uy \leq 1 \rceil,$$

$\psi(\rho^{-1}u)$ is in any case non-increasing quasiconvex in u and, provided ϕ is classical, it is non-decreasing concave in ρ, in which case also

$$\phi(x) = \min\lceil \psi(v) : vx \leq 1 \rceil.$$

The interpretation of the multiplier λ_t at x_t is that it is a support gradient of $\psi(\rho^{-1}u)$ at $\rho = 1$, that is

$$\psi(\rho^{-1}u_t) - \psi(u_t) \leq \lambda_t(\rho - 1).$$

Uniqueness of λ_t is equivalent to differentiability at $\rho = 1$, in which case

$$\frac{\partial \psi(\rho^{-1}u_t)}{\partial \rho}\bigg|_{\rho=1} = \lambda_t.$$

This shows the interpretation of the λ_t as marginal utilities, beside

the interpretation of the ϕ_t as utilities, in any solution of $S(\lambda, \phi)$.

Now let $\phi(x)$ be any classical utility function compatible

with the two demands. If ϕ_t is the value and g_t any support gradient

at x_t, so

$$\phi(x) - \phi_t \leq g_t(x - x_t),$$

then the compatibility condition

$$u_t x < 1 \Rightarrow \phi(x) \leq \phi_t$$

is equivalent to

$$g_t \leq \lambda_t u_t, \quad g_t x_t = \lambda_t, \quad \lambda_t > 0,$$

giving

$$\phi(x) - \phi_t \leq \lambda_t(u_t x - 1).$$

With $x = x_s$, therefore

$$\phi_s - \phi_t \leq \lambda_t D_{ts},$$

establishing the condition $S(\lambda, \phi)$, where the ϕ_t are the utility

levels at ϕ_t, and the λ_t are the Lagrangian multipliers. This shows

that these levels and multipliers constitute a multiplier-level solution

as formerly defined. Earlier it appeared that any multiplier-level solu-

tion can be so expressed in relation to some compatible classical utility.

Multiplier-level consistency S is thus identified with *classical consis-*

tency, that is the possibility of simultaneous compatibility with some

classical utility function. The condition C in Theorem 1.5 appears as

a restricted form of classical consistency, relative to a function of the

especially simple polyhedral type constructed under the condition S.

It has been concluded that various, and rather numerous, different forms of consistency condition which have been introduced for a pair of demands are in fact equivalent. The condition H has immediate intelligibility from usual terms of economic discussion, and K is of a type similar to the Houthakker condition in Samuelson's revealed preference approach to demand analysis. The others represent another departure, giving a technique for treating index questions as here and also more generally. But there is still another branch in the theory of consistency, treated next.

FIGURE 7

Classical Utility Construction

solution λ_r, ϕ_r: $\lambda_r > 0$, $\lambda_r(u_r x_s - 1) \geq \phi_s - \phi_r$
supports $\phi_r(x) = \phi_r + \lambda_r(u_r x - 1)$, function $\phi(x) = \min_r \phi_r(x)$
graph $t = \phi(x)$; catagraph $t \leq \phi(x)$
contour at level t: the x with $\phi(x) = t$

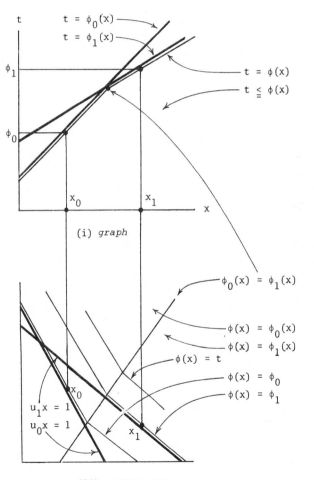

(i) *graph*

(ii) *contour map*

2. *Revealed choice and preference*

The importance of the demand data for the index problem is
that they put a constraint on permitted utilities by the requirement of
simultaneous compatibility. Consistency of the demands is the existence
of such permitted utilities, and several equivalent expressions of it
have been obtained, especially certain ones involving solution of linear
inequalities. Further such expressions will now appear of a different
type more connected with the "revealed" theory of Samuelson and general
ideas about choice.

Given any demand (x, p), there is always the possibility
though no necessity to view it as showing the choice of x from out of
the set

$$S = [y : py \leq px].$$

The possibility is simply because $x \in S$. The choice could instead have
been, for example, that of $(-px, x)$ out of the set

$$T = [(-M, y) : M \geq py],$$

or of any object a out of a set B where a and B are constructed
from (x, p) so that $a \in B$. There is no necessity for associating
(x, p) with the choice $(x; S)$, except that it happens to give language
for translating an already existing theory without altering it in any
way though it might give a different way of thinking about it. A similar
claim could be made for viewing (x, p) as showing the choice $[(-px, x);$
$T]$. This in fact corresponds to a more general theory from which the
$(x; S)$ theory results by imposing a limitation. But if there is resolu-
tion that (x, p) is to show the choice $(x; S)$, it can be declared by
calling $(x; S)$ the *revealed choice* of the demand (x, p). Then there

is the inevitable possibility, though again no necessity, of viewing any

choice hypothetically as expressing preferences, by the relation of the

chosen element to all the available elements. Thus the preferences in

the choice $(x; S)$ are

$$(x, S) = [(x, y) : y \in S].$$

The preferences in the revealed choice of the demand can be called its

revealed preferences. The term is usually arrived at immediately without

any notice taken of the revealed choice. But if anything needs emphasis

as peculiarly "revealed" it is the choice. For it is nothing new that

any choice can freely be taken to show preferences, even if, to the extent

knowable, it just happened and really might have nothing to do with pref-

erences (like the "best of all possible worlds" of Dr. Pangloss, or the

social optimum of economists — Dr. Pangloss is on better ground, because

it is the only world we have, and he is only nicely pretending it is an

element of a recognized larger set and not really that there is a crite-

rion available to him which settles a real issue, but economists with

their model do not have the same reassuring vacuity but by abuse of lan-

guage and persistent repetition are making a serious and false innuendo).

If several given choices $(x_t; S_t)$ $(x_t \in S_t)$, are to be

gathered as belonging to a single system of choice, this can be expressed

by the presumption that the revealed preferences collected together, as

in the set

$$[(x, y) : x = x_t, \quad y \in S_t],$$

belong to the same hypothetical system of preferences. But a system of

preferences is transitive, so also the transitive closure of the collec-

tion must then belong to the same hypothetical system. This gives the principle that the revealed preferences of a collection of choices form

the order which is the transitive closure of the collection of their

revealed preferences. There would be nothing more to the matter, and no

possible result to the exercise in hypothesis, were not some further

"revelation" either slipped in or in any case brought into the matter.

This other component of revelation is that, beside a choice

$(x; S)$ giving revealed preferences (x, S), that is

$$[(x, y) : py \leqq px],$$

also it gives *revealed non-preferences*. The hypothetically revealed non-

preferences of Samuelson are

$$(S-x, x) = [(y, x) : py \leqq px, \quad y \neq x].$$

Here instead the revealed non-preferences will be fewer, and form the

smaller set

$$[(y, x) : py < px].$$

It is from the conflict of hypothetically revealed preferences and non-

preferences that contradictions can arise rejecting such hypothesis, and

the exclusion of such contradictions gives a consistency condition on the

demands, identical with that considered formerly, which permits the

hypothesis still to be entertained. Without the non-preferences there

can be no contradictions and nothing more to be said one way or the other,

and the "revealed preference approach" would be an empty ritual, just

another ingredient in familiar economic metaphysics.

As with the revealed choice matter, this non-preference aspect

of Samuelson's principle has been glossed over in the terminology and in

the thought around it. But, by uncovering it, modifications such as the one

adopted here and others suggest themselves and put the principle in a

further perspective.

3. *Preference-nonpreference contradiction*

Let relations W, I, $V \subset \Omega^n \times \Omega_n$ be defined by

$$xWu \equiv ux \leq 1, \quad xIu \equiv ux = 1, \quad xVu \equiv ux < 1,$$

and say the bundle x is *within, on* or *under* the budget u correspondingly.

Since $u_t x_t = 1$, so $x_t \in Wu_t$, $(x_t ;. Wu_t)$ is a choice determined by (x_t, u_t), defining the *revealed choice* of the demand. Then

$$
\begin{aligned}
R_t &= (x_t, Wu_t) \\
&= [(x_t, x) : xWu_t] \\
&= [(x_t, x) : u_t x \leq 1] \\
&= [(x_t, x) : p_t x \leq p_t x_t]
\end{aligned}
$$

is the preference relation for the choice, defining the *revealed preference* relation of the demand. Then the revealed preference relation for the two demands simultaneously is the transitive closure

$$R_{01} = R_0 \overset{\rightarrow}{\cup} R_1$$

of the union of their two revealed preference relations.

The *revealed non-preference* relation of demand t is

$$
\begin{aligned}
N_t &= (Vu_t, x_t) \\
&= [(x, x_t) : xVu_t] \\
&= [(x, x_t) : u_t x < 1] \\
&= [(x, x_t) : p_t x < p_t x_t].
\end{aligned}
$$

For the two demands simultaneously it is

$$N_{01} = N_0 \cup N_1.$$

The absence of *revealed contradictions,* that is of contradictions between revealed preferences and revealed non-preferences, or the condition of revealed non-contradiction, requires

$$R_{01} \cap N_{01} = 0$$

or equivalently $R_{01} \subset \overline{N}_{01}$.

The relation R_{01} and N_{01} are, from their definitions, such that

$$xR_{01}y \iff (\vee s, t = 0, 1) \quad x = x_s, \quad u_s x_t \leqq 1, \quad u_t y \leqq 1.$$

$$xN_{01}y \iff (\vee t = 0, 1) \quad u_t x < 1, \quad y = x_t.$$

Thus the consistency condition $xR_{01}y \Rightarrow \sim xN_{01}y$ is equivalent to

$$u_s x_t \leqq 1, \quad u_t x_s \leqq 1 \Rightarrow u_t x_s \geqq 1$$

for all s, $t = 0$, 1. But this is equivalent to

$$u_0 x_1 \leqq 1, \quad u_1 x_0 \leqq 1 \Rightarrow u_0 x_1 = 1, \quad u_1 x_0 = 1,$$

which is the formerly considered condition K. Thus revealed consistency, as here introduced, is the same as all the consistencies which were formerly considered and shown to represent the same condition.

Had the revealed non-preference relation been taken instead to be

$$N_t = (Wu_t - x_t, \ x_t)$$

$$= [(x, \ x_t) : u_t x \leqq 1, \quad x \neq x_t],$$

the consistency condition obtained would have been

$$u_0 x_1 \leqq 1, \quad u_1 x_0 \leqq 1 \Rightarrow x_0 = x_1,$$

which is Samuelson's revealed preference condition K*.

The conclusion obtained above is as follows:

THEOREM 3.1   *If*

$$R_t = (x_t, \ Wu_t), \quad N_t = (Vu_t, \ x_t) \quad (t = 0, \ 1)$$

and

$$R_{01} = R_0 \overset{\rightarrow}{\cup} R_1, \quad N_{01} = N_0 \cup N_1$$

then

$$R_{01} \cap N_{01} = 0 \quad <=> \quad K.$$

That is, *the condition* K *is necessary and sufficient for the absence*
of revealed contradictions.

The revealed preference relation R_t of the demand t is
such that

$$xR_t y \quad <=> \quad x = x_t, \quad u_t y \leqq 1.$$

Then the cost-efficacy condition

$$H'_t(R) \equiv u_t x \leqq 1 => x_t R x$$

which is part of the condition $H_t(R)$ for compatibility between demand
t and any utility order R, can be restated as

$$R_t \subset R.$$

Hence the condition $H'(R)$ required by simultaneous compatibility is
equivalent to

$$R_0 \cup R_1 \subset R.$$

But with R transitive this is equivalent to

$$R_{01} \subset R.$$

Thus

$$H'(R) \quad <=> \quad R_{01} \subset R.$$

Also, the cost-efficiency condition is

$$H''(R) \equiv u_t x < 1 => x\bar{R}x_t$$

and this can be restated $N_t \subset \bar{R}.$ It follows that

$$H''(R) \quad <=> \quad N_{01} \subset R$$

and hence that

$$H(R) \quad <=> \quad R_{01} \subset R, \quad N_{01} \subset \bar{R}$$
$$<=> \quad R_{01} \subset R \subset \bar{N}_{01}.$$

Since, from Theorem 3.1,

$$K \quad <=> \quad R_{01} \subset \overline{N}_{01}$$
$$<=> \quad R_{01} \subset R_{01} \subset \overline{N}_{01},$$

this shows that

$$K \quad <=> \quad H(R_{01}).$$

But immediately

$$H(R_{01}) => H.$$

That the revealed preference relation of the demands itself be compatible with them simultaneously, and thus assure their consistency, can define their *revealed consistency*. Since it has been seen that also $H => K$, the following is now proved:

THEOREM 3.2 $H \quad <=> \quad H(R_{01}).$

That is, *there exists a utility order simultaneously compatible with the demands if and only if their revealed preference relation is one such order*, in other words revealed consistency is equivalent to general consistency.

4. Cost-efficiency and nonsatiation

It can be said there is *revealed cost-inefficiency* in period

t (t = 0, 1), relative to the demand observations in periods 0 and

1, if

$$xR_{01}x_t, \quad u_tx < 1 \quad \text{for some} \quad x,$$

which is to say, if there exists some bundle which is revealed as good as

the bundle purchased in the period but which, at the same prices, costs

less. The denial of this possibility defines *revealed cost-efficiency*.

This is the condition

$$xR_{01}x_t \Rightarrow u_tx \geqq 1$$

which immediately is identical with $H''(R_{01})$. But it has been seen,

since $H'(R)$ for any R is equivalent to $R_{01} \subset R$ and in any case

$R_{01} \subset R_{01}$, that $H'(R_{01})$ holds unconditionally. Accordingly,

$$H(R_{01}) \quad <=> \quad H''(R_{01}).$$

Thus there is the following, which gives still another view of the con-

sistency condition.

THEOREM 4.1   *Revealed consistency is equivalent to revealed cost-*

efficiency.

Yet another view is obtained as follows. If for some x, y

$$xR_{01}y, \quad x < y,$$

it can be said there is *revealed satiation* at x and *revealed oversatia-*

tion at y. The denial of such a possibility, defining *revealed non-*

satiation, is stated by

$$xR_{01}y \Rightarrow x \not< y$$

or by

$$R_{01} \subset \overline{\oslash}.$$

THEOREM 4.2 $R_{01} \subset \overline{\bigcirc}$ <=> K.

Since K has already been established as one of the many
statements of consistency, this shows that revealed non-satiation is yet
another.

Suppose the contrary of the left side. This is equivalent to

$$x_t R_{01} x, \quad x_t < x$$

for some t, x and then to

$$u_t x_s \leqq 1, \quad u_s x \leqq 1, \quad x_t < x$$

for some s, t, x. But since $u_s \geq 0$, so

$$x_t < x \Rightarrow u_s x_t < u_s x,$$

this implies

$$u_t x_s \leqq 1, \quad u_s x_t < 1$$

for some s, t and this is contrary to K. Also there is the converse,
since $u_s x_t < 1$ implies

$$u_s x \leqq 1, \quad x_t < x \quad \text{for some} \quad x.$$

This proves the theorem.

It has already been seen, in Section 1, that general consistency H is equivalent to classical consistency C. Since a classical
utility function is semi-increasing and therefore without satiation, a
conclusion from this is that H is equivalent to non-satiation consistency T defined by

$$T \equiv H(R), \quad R \subset \overline{\bigcirc} \quad \text{for some} \quad R.$$

But from here there is a more specific conclusion

$$
\begin{aligned}
H \quad &<=> \quad H(R_{01}) \\
&<=> \quad R_{01} \subset \overline{\bigcirc} \\
&<=> \quad H(R_{01}), \quad R_{01} \subset \overline{\bigcirc} \\
&\Rightarrow \quad T \\
&\Rightarrow \quad H.
\end{aligned}
$$

5. *Critical costs*

Consider the critical cost functions $\hat{\rho}$, $\check{\rho}$ applied to the revealed preference relation R_{01}, and for r, s = 0, 1 the values

$$\hat{\rho}_{rs} = \hat{\rho}(u_r, x_s), \quad \check{\rho}_{rs} = \check{\rho}(u_r, x_s)$$

defining *revealed critical costs*. Thus, from the definitions of these functions and of the relation, they are

$$\hat{\rho}_{rs} = \inf[u_r x : x R_{01} x_s]$$

$$= \min[u_r x_t : x_t R_{01} x_s]$$

$$= \min[u_r x_t : u_t x_s \leq 1]$$

and

$$\check{\rho}_{rs} = \inf[u_r x : x_s \overline{R}_{01} x]$$

$$= \inf[u_r x : u_s x_t \leq 1 \Rightarrow u_t x > 1]$$

$$= \min[u_r x : u_s x_t \leq 1 \Rightarrow u_t x \geq 1].$$

Since $u_t x_t = 1$ it follows that

$$\hat{\rho}_{rs} \leq u_r x_s,$$

in particular,

$$\hat{\rho}_{rr} \leq 1,$$

and also

$$\check{\rho}_{rr} \geq 1.$$

THEOREM 5.1 $\hat{\rho}_{rs} = u_r x_s$ $(r \neq s)$.

Thus, with $r \neq s$,

$$\hat{\rho}_{rs} = \min[u_r x_t : u_t x_s \leq 1],$$

so if $u_r x_s \leq 1$, so that the range of t is $\{r, s\}$, then

$$\hat{\rho}_{rs} = \min[u_r x_r, \ u_r x_s]$$

$$= \min[1, \ u_r x_s]$$

$$= u_r x_s$$

and if $u_r x_s > 1$, so that the range of t is just r, then

$$\hat{\rho}_{rs} = \min[u_r x_s] = u_r x_s.$$

Thus in any case $\hat{\rho}_{rs} = u_r x_s$.

THEOREM 5.2   K $<=>$ $\hat{\rho}_{rr} = u_r x_r$.

Thus,

$$\hat{\rho}_{rr} = \min[u_r x_t : u_t x_r \leq 1],$$

so if $u_r x_s > 1$ (s $\neq$ r) then

$$\hat{\rho}_{rr} = \min[u_r x_r] = u_r x_r.$$

Also if $u_s x_r \leq 1$ then

$$\hat{\rho}_{rr} = \min[u_r x_r, \ u_r x_s],$$

in which case

$$\hat{\rho}_{rr} = u_r x_r \quad <=> \quad u_r x_s \geq 1.$$

Thus

$$u_s x_r \leq 1 \Rightarrow u_r x_s \geq 1$$

if and only if

$$\hat{\rho}_{rr} = u_r x_r.$$

But the first condition is equivalent to K.

COROLLARY   K $<=>$ $\hat{\rho}_{rs} = u_r x_s$.

This follows by combination with the previous theorem.

The present theorem gives a connection with Theorem 4.1. For

$$H''_t(R_{01}) \quad <=> \quad x R_{01} x_t \Rightarrow u_t x \geq 1$$

$$<=> \quad \inf[u_t x : x R_{01} x_t] \geq 1$$

$$<=> \quad \hat{\rho}_{tt} \geq 1,$$

and it has already been remarked that $\hat{\rho}_{tt} \leq 1$, unconditionally. Hence

$$H''(R_{01}) \quad <=> \quad \hat{\rho}_{tt} = 1$$

$$<=> \quad K \quad (\text{Theorem 5.2})$$

$$\Longleftrightarrow \quad H \quad \text{(Theorem 1.5)}$$

$$\Longleftrightarrow \quad H(R_{01}) \quad \text{(Theorem 3.2)}$$

THEOREM 5.3 $\overset{v}{\rho}_{rr} \leqq \overset{\wedge}{\rho}_{rr} \Rightarrow K \Rightarrow \overset{v}{\rho}_{rs} \leqq \overset{\wedge}{\rho}_{rs}.$

Thus, K implies

$$u_{sr} \leqq 1 \Rightarrow u_r x_s \geqq 1,$$

which implies

$$\overset{v}{\rho}_{rs} = \min[u_r x : u_s x_t \leqq 1 \Rightarrow u_t x \geqq 1]$$

$$\leqq u_r x_s.$$

But, by Theorem 5.2, Corollary, K also implies $\overset{\wedge}{\rho}_{rs} = u_r x_s.$ Thus K

implies $\overset{v}{\rho}_{rs} \leqq \overset{\wedge}{\rho}_{rs}.$ Alternatively, K is equivalent to $R_{01} \subset \overline{\mathfrak{S}},$ by

Theorem 4.2, and this implies $\overset{v}{\rho} \leqq \overset{\wedge}{\rho},$ by the Theorem of Ch. I, Sec. 3.

To prove the remaining part of the theorem, suppose K does not hold, say

$$u_s x_r \leqq 1, \quad u_r x_s < 1.$$

Then

$$\overset{\wedge}{\rho}_{rr} = \min[u_r x_t : x_t R_{01} x_1]$$

$$= \min[u_r x_s, \quad u_r x_r]$$

$$= u_r x_s < 1.$$

But then also

$$\overset{v}{\rho}_{rr} = \min[u_r x : u_r x_t \leqq 1 \Rightarrow u_t x \geqq 1]$$

$$= \min[u_r x : u_r x \geqq 1, \quad u_s x \geqq 1]$$

$$\geqq 1,$$

so $\overset{\wedge}{\rho}_{rr} < \overset{v}{\rho}_{rr},$ and the theorem is proved.

Alternatively, it is always the case that

$$\overset{\wedge}{\rho}_{rr} \leqq 1 \leqq \overset{v}{\rho}_{rr}.$$

But if K does not hold then, as just seen, $\overset{\wedge}{\rho}_{rr} < 1$ for some $r,$

whence the required conclusion.

Concerning the general formula for $\breve{\rho}_{rs}$ it should be noted that if $u_s x_r \leqq 1$ it gives

$$\breve{\rho}_{rs} = \min[u_r x : u_r x \geqq 1, \ u_s x \geqq 1]$$

and if $u_s x_r > 1$ it gives

$$\breve{\rho}_{rs} = \min[u_r x : u_s x \geqq 1].$$

But in the first case, if $u_s \leqq u_r$, so that $u_s x \geqq 1$ implies $u_r x \geqq 1$, the second formula is again valid, and otherwise

$$\breve{\rho}_{rs} = 1.$$

This shows the following:

THEOREM 5.4   If $u_s x_r > 1$ or $u_s \leqq u_r$ then

$$\breve{\rho}_{rs} = \min[u_r x : u_s x \geqq 1]$$

and otherwise

$$\breve{\rho}_{rs} = 1.$$

6. *Revealed bounds and classical limits*

With the critical cost functions $\hat{\rho}$, $\check{\rho}$ now determined in respect to any utility order R, define

$$\hat{\rho}_{rs}(R) = \hat{\rho}(u_r, x_s), \quad \check{\rho}_{rs}(R) = \check{\rho}(u_r, x_s),$$

so

$$\hat{\rho}_{rs} = \hat{\rho}_{rs}(R_{10}), \quad \check{\rho}_{rs} = \check{\rho}_{rs}(R_{10}).$$

For any R which is complete and without satiation $\check{\rho} = \hat{\rho}$, so in that case both functions can be denoted ρ. In particular $\check{\rho}_{rs}(R) = \hat{\rho}_{rs}(R)$, and these are denoted $\rho_{rs}(R)$.

THEOREM 6.1   *With* (x_t, u_t) $(u_t x_t = 1)$ *given for* $t = 0, 1$ *and*

$$\hat{\rho}_{rs} = u_r x_s, \quad \check{\rho}_{rs} = \min[u_r x : u_s x_t \leq 1 \Rightarrow u_t x \geq 1],$$

for any utility order R

$$H(R) \Rightarrow \check{\rho}_{rs} \leq \check{\rho}_{rs}(R), \quad \hat{\rho}_{rs}(R) \leq \hat{\rho}_{rs},$$

so if R *is complete and without satiation*

$$H(R) \Rightarrow \check{\rho}_{rs} \leq \rho_{rs}(R) \leq \hat{\rho}_{rs}.$$

This follows from Theorem 5.2, and from the Theorem in Ch. I, Sec. 3, Corollary (iii), since $H(R) \Rightarrow R_{01} \subset R$.

THEOREM 6.2   *For any* $\lambda = (\lambda_0, \lambda_1)$, $\phi = (\phi_0, \phi_1)$ *let*

$$\phi_t(x) = \phi_t + \lambda_t(u_t x - 1)$$

and

$$\phi(x) = \min_t \phi_t(x).$$

Also let

$$\rho_{rs}(\lambda, \phi) = \rho_{rs}(R),$$

where R *is the relation represented by the classical utility function* $\phi(x)$ *thus determined from* λ, ϕ *and let* $S(\lambda, \phi)$ *be the condition*

$$\lambda_t > 0, \quad \lambda_s D_{st} \geq \phi_t - \phi_s,$$

so this implies $H(R)$. *Then the values of* $\rho_{rs}(\lambda, \phi)$ *for all* λ, ϕ

subject to $S(\lambda, \phi)$ *cover all points of the closed interval with upper*

and lower limits given by the numbers $\overset{\wedge}{\rho}_{rs}, \overset{\vee}{\rho}_{rs}$ *with the possible*

exception of the lower limit.

With $\phi(x)$ determined as stated,

$$\rho_{rs}(\lambda, \phi) = \min[u_r x : \phi(x) \geq \phi(x_s)].$$

But $S(\lambda, \phi)$ implies $\phi(x_s) = \phi_s$, so

$$\phi(x) \geq \phi(x_s) \quad <=> \quad \phi(x) \geq \phi_s$$

$$<=> \quad \phi_t + \lambda_t(u_t x - 1) \geq \phi_s$$

$$<=> \quad u_t x \geq 1 + \frac{\phi_s - \phi_t}{\lambda_t},$$

and hence

$$\rho_{rs}(\lambda, \phi) = \min[u_r x : u_t x \geq 1 + \frac{\phi_s - \phi_t}{\lambda_t}].$$

There is no alteration of the matter if there is restriction

to solutions with $\lambda_s = 1$, $\phi_s = 0$. Then $S(\lambda, \phi)$ becomes equivalent to

$$\lambda_r > 0, \quad u_s x_r - 1 \geq \phi_r \geq -\lambda_r(u_r x_s - 1),$$

and

$$\rho_{rs}(\lambda, \phi) = \min[u_r x : u_s x \geq 1, \quad u_r x \geq 1 - \frac{\phi_r}{\lambda_r}].$$

First it will be shown that a solution λ, ϕ can be chosen

to make $\rho_{rs}(\lambda, \phi) = u_r x_s$. Thus, if any solutions λ, ϕ exist, as they

must under the condition K, λ_r must satisfy

$$u_s x_r - 1 \geq -\lambda_r(u_r x_s - 1).$$

Then it is permissible to take

$$\phi_r = -\lambda_r(u_r x_s - 1),$$

so

$$1 - \frac{\phi_r}{\lambda_r} = u_r x_s,$$

and

$$\rho_{rs}(\lambda, \phi) = \min[u_r x : u_s x \geq 1, \quad u_r x \geq u_r x_s].$$

Immediately

$$\rho_{rs}(\lambda, \phi) \geq u_r x_s.$$

But because $u_s x_s = 1$ also

$$\rho_{rs}(\lambda, \phi) \leq u_r x_s.$$

Hence

$$\rho_{rs}(\lambda, \phi) = u_r x_s.$$

But by Theorem 5.2, Corollary, K implies

$$\hat{\rho}_{rs} = u_r x_s.$$

Thus

$$\rho_{rs}(\lambda, \phi) = \hat{\rho}_{rs}.$$

Now it will be shown that a solution λ, ϕ can be chosen to make $\rho_{rs}(\lambda, \phi)$ arbitrarily close to $\check{\rho}_{rs}$. Cases permitted by K will be distinguished as follows:

$$(1) \qquad u_s x_r \leq 1, \quad u_r x_s \geq 1,$$

otherwise

$$(2) \qquad u_s x_r > 1$$

with subcases

$$(2.1) \qquad u_r x_s \geq 1$$

$$(2.2) \qquad u_r x_s < 1.$$

In case (1) the formula for $\check{\rho}_{rs}$ gives

$$\check{\rho}_{rs} = \min[u_r x : u_r x \geq 1, \quad u_s x \geq 1].$$

and in case (2) it gives

$$\check{\rho}_{rs} = \min[u_r x : u_s x \geq 1].$$

In case (1) it is permissible to take $\phi_r = u_s x_r - 1$ and λ_r arbitrarily large. As $\lambda_r \to \infty$, $\rho_{rs}(\lambda, \phi)$ is non-increasing and converges to $\check{\rho}_{rs}$.

More specifically, if $u_s x_r = 1$ it is constant and identical with $\breve{\rho}_{rs}$,

and if $u_s x_r < 1$ its behaviour is the same as

$$\rho_{rs}(\varepsilon) = \min[u_r x : u_s x \geq 1, \ u_r x \geq 1 + \varepsilon]$$

for $\varepsilon > 0$, as $\varepsilon \to 0$. Thus if $(1 + \varepsilon)u_s \leq u$ for some $\varepsilon > 0$ then

$\rho_{rs}(\varepsilon) = \breve{\rho}_{rs}$ for this and all smaller ε, so the value $\breve{\rho}_{rs}$ is cer-

tainly attained. Otherwise $\rho_{rs}(\varepsilon) = 1 + \varepsilon$ while $\breve{\rho}_{rs} = 1$, so

$\rho_{rs}(\varepsilon) > \breve{\rho}_{rs}$, and the value $\breve{\rho}_{rs}$ is approached only in the limit.

　　　In case 2.1 it is permissible to take $\phi_r = u_s x_r - 1$ and

arbitrary $\lambda_r > 0$. Then it is possible to choose λ_r so that $0 < \lambda_r \leq$

ϕ_r, making $1 - \dfrac{\phi_r}{\lambda_r} \leq 0$, so there is the reduction

$$\rho_{rs}(\lambda, \phi) = \min[u_r x : u_s x \geq 1],$$

because of redundancy of the second constraint. But in case 2, also

$\breve{\rho}_{rs}$ is given by this formula, showing that $\rho_{rs} = \breve{\rho}_{rs}$.

　　　In case 2.2 it is permissible to take ϕ_r as before and then

any λ_r such that

$$0 < \lambda_r \leq \min[\phi_r, \ \phi_r/(1 - u_r x_s)].$$

Then again, because the same constraint becomes redundant the formula

reduces as before and gives the same conclusion.

　　　It remains to remark that the solutions under the condition

$S(\lambda, \phi)$ form a convex, that is linearly connected, set and $\rho(\lambda, \phi)$ is

a continuous function on this set, so its values form a connected set.

But the only connected sets of real numbers are intervals.

THEOREM 6.3　*The values of* $\rho_{rs}(R)$ *for all complete and non-satiated*

R *subject to* H(R) *describe all the points in the closed interval with*

upper and lower limits $\hat{\rho}_{rs}$, $\check{\rho}_{rs}$ *with the possible exception of* $\check{\rho}_{rs}$.

　　　This follows by combination of Theorems 6.1 and 6.2. Thus

Theorem 6.1 shows the values must all lie within this interval. Then

Theorem 6.2 shows that even with further classical restriction on R all

values in the interval can be attained except possibly the lower limit.

The exception is possible only if $u_s x_r \leq 1$ and there is no $\varepsilon > 0$ such

that $(1 + \varepsilon)u_s \leq u_r$.

FIGURE 8

Cost of Living Limits

limits of cost of 0-utility at 1-prices
for all compatible utilities
consistent cases

(i) $u_0 x_1 < 1$, $u_1 x_0 > 1$: (a) $u_1 \not> u_0$ (b) $u_1 > u_0$
(ii) $u_0 x_1 > 1$, $u_1 x_0 > 1$
(iii) $u_1 x_0 < 1$, $u_0 x_1 > 1$

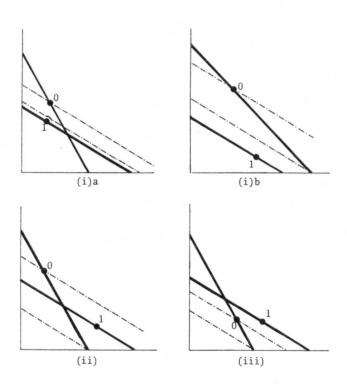

(i)a   (i)b

(ii)   (iii)

FIGURE 9

Utility for Upper Limits

limiting positions of 0-utility locus
for upper limits of cost of 0-utility at 1-prices
for all compatible utilities, cases as in figure 8

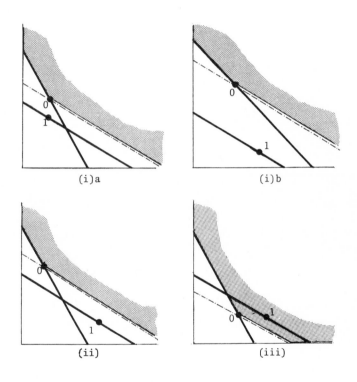

(i)a   (i)b

(ii)   (iii)

FIGURE 10

Utility for Lower Limits

limiting positions of 0-utility locus
for lower limits of cost of 0-utility at 1-prices
for all compatible utilities, cases as in figure 8

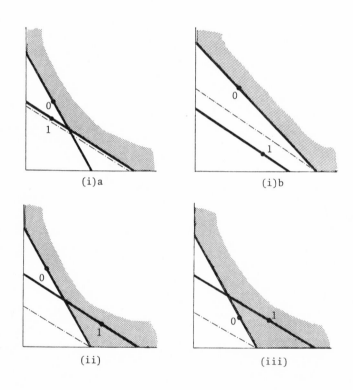

(i)a   (i)b

(ii)   (iii)

III : THE HOMOGENEOUS PROBLEM — LASPEYRES AND PAASCHE

Introduction

Anywhere in economics, in everyday statistics or in volumes
of theory, it is easy to meet price indices. They are introduced as such.
But still, how could it be known if any identity happened to be a mistake,
or how this should matter? No plain answer is given. But still, it is
possible to make enquiries. Is 1.6 a price index? To some this is just
a number. Then does it become a price index if it is called one?
Perhaps. Then is any number a price index? At this point there is a
stop and disengagement. But try again. Is $p_1 x_0 / p_0 x_0$ a price index?
Yes, of course, that is the Laspeyres price index! But why is it a
price index?.... The story of this encounter is — though because of a
scatter of formulae it has an air of better science — much the same as
the previous one.

Irving Fisher lists (by my count) 126 price index formulae,
which he describes, compares and classifies as a botanist might wild
flowers. (Out of respect for empiricism it should be stated that
Dr. Yrjö O. Vartia, of the Research Institute of the Finnish Economy,
counts 145.) By "crossing", new price indices can be bred from others,
some with especially desirable, even "ideal" properties, and their
variety has no limit. But none was produced which met the "Tests"
Fisher required for the "true" index; it can still be asked what would
have been settled if one, or many, had been found.

The index-number-making which had a culmination with
Irving Fisher still flourishes. But next to it is a theory which has
become regarded as more modern, dealing with so-called "constant utility"

index numbers. These are index numbers derived on the assumption
(which could be impossible with the data) that demand is governed by a
utility function and, moreover, the function has some special form.
Here there is a change. Formerly, it was as if an answer was proposed
without first having had a question, and it was wondered if it could be
an answer to a question, any question at all. Even, many answers to no
question in particular were proposed — the names of their proposers are
attached to some of them. Now a question comes first and the answer
follows. It is easy, and even usual, to overlook a possible vacuity:
the assumption which gives basis for the question asked of the data —
for which an answer has been deduced on condition there is an answer —
can be impossible with the data, so in fact there is no proper question
and no answer. Nevertheless the order of question and answer is more
natural — unless there never is notice whether one stands on clear
ground or sinks in quagmires of irresolution, as sometimes fits a well-
conditioned theoretical economist. Buscheguennce (a French translation
of Byushgens), with his remark about Fisher's ideal index and homogeneous
quadratic utility, the subject of the next chapter , possibly initiated
the "constant-utility" approach to price indices; at least, he made a
distinct contribution to it. The Cobb-Douglas utility function is
similarly related to Palgrave's price-index. The "New Formula" of Wald
(1939), which involves quadratic utility, is a more general, direct
descendant of Buscheguennce, as also is a related still more general
formula of Afriat. But these apply to the broader "cost of living"
problem, which was the concern in the last chapter and does not of
necessity show anything about price indices. The Klein-Rubin cost of

living index is related to Palgrave's price index in the same way that
Wald's formula is related to Fisher's; or it would be, were an account
given of the parameter which appears in it as a constant of integration.

Examples of the approach involving utility of a special
algebraical form, and leading to an algebraical formula for an index in
terms of the demand data alone, are so few as hardly to constitute an
important general approach. Also, they are special in a way which is
linked, on main appearances, more with accidental niceties of algebra
than with any central theoretical purpose. The example dealt with in
the next chapter, which involves quadratic utility, gives expression to
the typical features of the approach. One feature which seems never to
be noticed, but should nevertheless be recognized as outstanding, is that
the basic hypothesis can be inadmissible on the data. The conclusion
obtained with quadratics is striking enough and also unimportant enough
not to be altogether spoilt by neglect of its possible vacuity. But,
less satisfactorily, there has been neglect of the same matter for price
indices generally, free of arbitrary restrictions on the form of utility
and incorporating just the particular restriction which is characteristic
of a price index as such.

A proposition which has been most central for the theory of
price indices makes the Laspeyres and Paasche indices upper and lower
"limits" of the "true index". Two arguments offer this: one is well
known from textbooks, and the other is familiar from Keynes. Then
follows the "theorem" that the Paasche index does not exceed that of
Laspeyres. The inequality is not generally valid; rather, it has been
deduced under a restrictive hypothesis, which needs to be excavated out

of the argument used in the deduction. The "limits" are in the sense of

bounds, not of best possible bounds for which there has yet been no

argument. The meaning of "true index" is, at least in the present

context, still left loose; it can be allowed that the index either is

unique, or capable of many, or even of no values; in any case, it

describes a set of values, which must be a function of the pair of

demands (x_0, p_0), (x_1, p_1) since everything has reference to these. The

"limits" proposition appears to say this set is bounded from above and

below by the Laspeyres and Paasche indices. Should "true index" be

properly defined, the set should be describable better than this.

There is even no assurance yet that it is ever non-empty. The descrip-

tion of the set is complete in at least one particular case: if the

Paasche index exceeds that of Laspeyres it is empty; or, contrapositively,

if a "true index" exists then the Paasche index does not exceed the

Laspeyres index. This last conclusion gives the form of a possible

theorem, and it would be one were a definite meaning given to the

hypothesis in it. And then there could be enquiry about the converse:

if the Paasche index does not exceed the Laspeyres index then does a

"true index" exist? The question is never asked. If no "true index"

exists, still the "limits" proposition, taught on limitless blackboards,

does have that guarantee of veracity by which it is always permitted

to say anything about nothing. But it could have a vacuity, and if this

is to be avoided at least a "true index" must be shown to exist. The

possible values have been limited to lie somewhere between the Paasche

and Laspeyres indices, that is on the closed interval with these as its

lower and upper extremities. In the search for favourable candidates it seems especially interesting to know whether either of the Paasche

and Laspeyres indices themselves is a true index. For though they are

always called "price indices", it is not said why, or whether they are

"true" or not. These possibilities are extreme, and between them lies

their geometric mean which is the Fisher ideal index. It has been said

that this must be a "better approximation" to a "true index" than either

extreme. No reason is given; nor can there be one before even the

existence, let alone the actual identity, of what is being approximated

is known.

An examination of familiar arguments for the "limits"

proposition will give evidences about the meaning of "true index", and

show hypotheses which produce first that proposition and then the usual

Paasche-Laspeyres inequality.

In the textbook argument, or an approximation of it, an

indifference curve is drawn through the point x_0 in such a way that it

touches the budget line $p_0 x = p_0 x_0$. This signifies that there is

consideration of some utility order R which is compatible with the

demand (x_0, p_0). So, with

$$\rho(p,x) = \min[py : yRx]$$

as the associated utility-cost function, there is the condition

(0) $\rho(p_0, x_0) = p_0 x_0.$

Thus R is constrained to represent $p_0 x_0$ as not merely the cost of x_0

but as the cost of the utility of x_0, at prices p_0. Then there is

consideration of the cost $\rho(p_1, x_0)$ of the utility of x_0 at the prices

p_1, and it is observed that

$$\rho(p_1, x_0) \leqq p_1 x_0.$$

The observation usually is made by reference to the diagram, but all that is relevant is the reflexivity of R. For this assures that one way of purchasing the utility of x_0 is by purchasing x_0 itself, at the cost $p_1 x_0$, so the cost, that is the minimum cost $\rho(p_1, x_0)$, of purchasing that utility cannot exceed that cost. Then there is the conclusion

(10) $$\rho(p_1, x_0)/\rho(p_0, x_0) \leqq p_1 x_0/p_0 x_0.$$

Similarly, if R is constrained also by compatibility with the demand (x_1, p_1), so

(1) $$\rho(p_1, x_1) = p_1 x_1,$$

then, since in any case

$$\rho(p_1, x_0) \leqq p_1 x_0,$$

there is the conclusion

(01) $$\rho(p_0, x_1)/\rho(p_1, x_1) \leqq p_0 x_1/p_1 x_1.$$

Thus *the simultaneous compatibility of R with the demands in the two periods* 0 *and* 1 *gives the conclusions* (10) and (01). The argument is that $(0) \Rightarrow (10)$ and $(1) \Rightarrow (01)$, and hence

$$(0) \text{ and } (1) \quad \Rightarrow \quad (10) \text{ and } (01)$$

That is as far as the argument can go without imposition of a further feature.

A statement of that needed further feature, usually without mention, is that R is supposed to be such as to make the proportion

$$\rho(p_0, x) : \rho(p_1, x)$$

independent of x; thus,

$$\rho(p_1, x) = P_{10}\rho(p_0, x)$$

and inversely

$$\rho(p_0, x) = P_{01}\rho(p_1, x),$$

P_{10} and P_{01} being independent of x and such that

$$P_{10}P_{01} = 1.$$

Here enters the idea of a price index P_{10} as giving the slope of a homogeneous linear relation $M_1 = P_{10}M_0$ between incomes M_0, M_1 which at prices p_0, p_1 have the same purchasing power, that is, which purchase the same utility. In particular, with $x = x_0$,

$$\rho(p_1, x_0)/\rho(p_0, x_0) = P_{10}$$

and then with (10),

$$P_{10} \leqq P_0 x_1/P_0 x_0.$$

Similarly

$$P_{01} \leqq P_0 x_1/P_1 x_1.$$

Then, because

$$P_{10} = P_{01}^{-1},$$

it follows that

$$P_1 x_1/P_0 x_1 \leqq P_{10} \leqq P_1 x_0/P_0 x_0.$$

The price index P_{10} thus has the Laspeyres and Paasche indices as upper and lower bounds.

The price index P_{10} is determined by the utility order R and the prices p_0, p_1. The condition on R which permits this determination, for arbitrary p_0 and p_1, is equivalent to the requirement that the utility-cost function admit the factorization into a product

$$\rho(p, x) = \theta(p)\phi(x),$$

of price and quantity functions. Then the price index, with 0 and 1 as base and current periods, is expressed as the ratio

$$P_{10} = P_1/P_0$$

of "price-levels"

$$P_0 = \theta(p_0), \quad P_1 = \theta(p_1).$$

Keynes had a different argument. It is assumed that any £ at prices p_0 purchases a bundle of good e_0, where $p_0 e_0 = 1$. Then £M_0 purchases M_0 of these, that is the bundle $e_0 M_0$. In other words, the expansion locus for prices p_0 is the ray through e_0, the demand with an income M_0 at these prices being the point $e_0 M_0$ on the ray. Similarly, any £ at prices p_1 purchases a bundle of goods e_1, where $p_1 e_1 = 1$, and £M_1 purchases the bundle $e_1 M_1$.

Let R be a utility order which is compatible with the given demands $(e_0 M_0, p_0)$, $(e_1 M_1, p_1)$ for all M_0, M_1. In other words, R is compatible with the expansion loci for prices p_0, p_1 being rays through e_0, e_1. These rays could be specified by any points x_0, x_1 on them. Then

$$e_0 = x_0 (p_0 x_0)^{-1}, \quad e_1 = x_1 (p_1 x_1)^{-1};$$

so

$$p_1 e_0 = p_1 x_0 / p_0 x_0$$

is the Laspeyres index, with 0 and 1 as base and current periods, and

$$1/p_0 e_1 = p_1 x_1 / p_0 x_1$$

is the Paasche index.

Consider incomes M_0, M_1 which are decided by R to have the same purchasing power at prices p_0, p_1. Since, governed by R, the incomes purchase the bundles $e_0 M_0$, $e_1 M_1$ the condition is that these bundles be decided indifferent by R. Should

$$p_1 e_0 M_0 < M_1,$$

it would follow (by "revealed preference") that $e_1 M_1$ is superior to $e_0 M_0$, and not indifferent; so this is impossible. Hence

$$M_1 / M_0 \leqq p_1 e_0,$$

and similarly

$$M_0 / M_1 \leqq p_0 e_1,$$

giving

$$1/p_0 e_1 \leqq M_1 / M_0 \leqq p_1 e_0$$

equivalently

$$p_1 x_1 / p_0 x_1 \leqq M_1 / M_0 \leqq p_1 x_0 / p_1 x_1,$$

where x_0, x_1 are any points on the rays through e_0, e_1.

The conclusions of the two arguments are different, and so are the assumptions. Keynes remarked his argument to be "more rigorous", but both, when all that is thought or half-thought is said, are certainly simple and rigorous. However, while the textbook argument explicitly deals with a utility order with the restrictive property which immediately permits definition of a price index, Keynes' argument does not. This makes the textbook argument more directly to the point, though both arguments have been inarticulate about that point.

In both arguments the utility order which is to be the

criterion for purchasing power is restricted to have simultaneous
compatibility with the given pair of demands for periods 0, 1. But each
requires a different additional restriction. With one, the price index
makes an immediate appearance as the ratio, which is fixed by assumption,
between incomes in the two periods which have the same purchasing power.
With the other, expansion loci in the two periods are assumed to be rays
from the origin in the commodity space, and there is no explicit entry
of the idea of a price. The conclusion in the first argument is that
the price index is bounded by the Paasche and Laspeyres indices, and of
the second it is that the ratio of equivalent incomes is bounded in the
same way.

The conclusion of the first, from the definition of the
price index, implies that of the second. That of the second should there
be a price index would imply that of the first. But the second argument
tells nothing of there being a price index. There is a proper difference
between the two arguments. But either gives the conclusion that if a
utility order exists subject to the restrictions required in it then the
Paasche index does not exceed the Laspeyres index. This conclusion,
familiar as the index number "Theorem", can be stated $P \leqq L$. Let the
two hypotheses which have been seen to give this be denoted H_I, H_{II}; so

$$H_I \;\Rightarrow\; P \leqq L, \quad H_{II} \;\Rightarrow\; P \leqq L.$$

Consider a utility order R with the property

$$xRy \;\Rightarrow\; x\lambda Ry\lambda \quad (\lambda \geqq 0),$$

by which it is homogeneous, or conical. For such an order it is
immediate and elementary that the relation between equivalent incomes,

at different prices, is described by a price index; that is, it is

homogeneous linear; and also all expansion paths are rays. Thus the

requirement that R be such a type of relation strengthens both of

restrictions on R which appear in the two arguments as additional to

the requirement of simultaneous compatibility with the given pair of

demands. Let H_0 assert the existence of such a homogeneous R which is

simultaneously compatible with the demands, defining their *homogeneous*

consistency, so now

$$H_0 \Rightarrow H_I, \quad H_0 \Rightarrow H_{II}.$$

It is shown, in this chapter, that

$$H_0 \Leftrightarrow P \leqq L,$$

and with this it follows here that

$$H_0 \Leftrightarrow H_I \Leftrightarrow H_{II} \Leftrightarrow P \leqq L.$$

Thus three properly different conditions on the pair of

demands, each requiring the existence of a compatible utility order

having one of three different properties, are seen to be equivalent to

each other and to the usual inequality between the Laspeyres and Paasche

indices. Here is one special context where three properly different

properties for a utility order lose their difference, and there are

others. For one instance — one which is tractable by differential

calculus methods — if a utility order is considered which determines a

continuously differentiable demand function then these three properties

are equivalent.

But anyway, without dependence on such outside propositions,

R in being conical satisfies simultaneously the additional restrictions

of both arguments. It is a greater restriction than either, and therefore the set of "true" indices associated with it, bounded between
Paasche and Laspeyres, can only be the same or smaller than in the other
two instances. But it is shown later in this chapter that the set
exhausts the entire closed interval between those extremities. The other
two sets, being the same or larger, and bounded in the same interval,
can only coincide with it, and with that interval.

Any ambiguity about "true index" from there being now three
different identifications shows no effect in the unambiguous result that
the set of values is in any case identical with the Paasche-Laspeyres
interval. The "true" points are just the points in that interval and no
others; and none is more true than another. There is no sense to a
point in the interval being a better approximation to "the true index"
than others. There is no proper distinction of "constant utility"
indices, since all these points have that distinction.

FIGURE 11

The "Limits" Argument

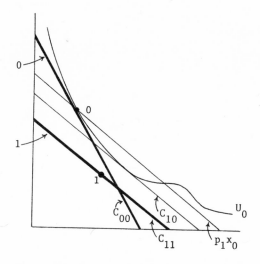

applying to demands for periods 0, 1
and any utility described by a utility-cost
function ρ

$p_0 x_0$ cost of 0-demand at 0-prices

$C_{00} = \rho(p_0, x_0)$ cost of 0-utility at 0-prices

$p_1 x_0$ cost of 0-demand at 1-prices

$C_{10} = \rho(p_1, x_0)$ cost of 0-utility at 1-prices

compatibility between 0-demand and utility
expressed by 0-cost line which simultaneously
touches 0-utility curve and passes through
0-demand point: $C_{00} = p_0 x_0$

in any case $C_{10} \leqq p_1 x_0$, so
$$C_{10}/C_{00} \leqq p_1 x_0/p_0 x_0$$
and the same with 0, 1 interchanged gives
$$C_{01}/C_{11} \leqq p_0 x_1/p_1 x_1$$

price-index introduced by the condition

$$\rho(p_1, x) = P_{10}\rho(p_0, x) \text{ for all } x$$

in particular for $x = x_0, x_1$

$$C_{10} = P_{10}C_{00}, \quad C_{11} = P_{10}C_{01}$$

conclusion:

$$p_1 x_1/p_0 x_1 \leqq P_{10} \leqq p_1 x_0/p_0 x_0.$$

FIGURE 12

Keynes' "Method of Limits"

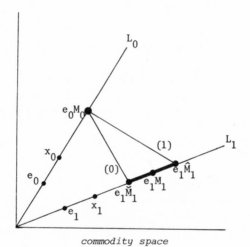

commodity space

e_0, e_1 bundles purchased by £1 at prices p_0, p_1 so

$$p_0 e_0 = 1, \quad p_1 e_1 = 1$$

x_0, x_1 arbitrary bundles purchased at prices p_0, p_1

$\hat{P}_{10} = p_1 e_0$ Laspeyres, $\check{P}_{10} = 1/p_0 e_1$ Paasche

for incomes M_0, M_1 with the same purchasing power

at prices p_0, p_1: $\check{P}_{10} \leqq M_1/M_0 \leqq \hat{P}_{10}$

FIGURE 13

The Paasche-Laspeyres Cone

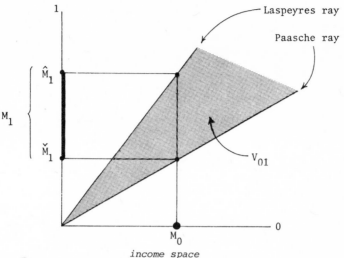

income space

M_0 any income at prices p_0

M_1 the equivalent income at prices p_1

indeterminate in the interval between

$$\hat{M}_1 = \hat{P}_{10}M_0, \quad \check{M}_1 = \check{P}_{10}M_0;$$

alternatively

$$M_1 = P_{10}M_0$$

where P_{10} is indeterminate in the interval

between $\hat{P}_{10}, \check{P}_{10}$; or again

$$(M_0, M_1) \in V_{01}$$

the graph of the correspondence being the

Paasche-Laspeyres cone V_{01}

1. Conical utility and expansion loci

A utility relation being given by a set $R \subset \Omega^n \times \Omega^n$, in the Cartesian product of the commodity space Ω^n with itself, the case of *homogeneous utility* is when this set is a cone. With conical R, if any point (x, y) is included then so is every point $(x, y)\lambda = (x\lambda, y\lambda)$ $(\lambda \geqq 0)$ on the ray through it,

$$(x, y) \in R \Rightarrow (x, y)\lambda \in R \quad (\lambda \geqq 0).$$

With the notation $xRy \equiv (x, y) \in R$, this condition is

$$xRy \Rightarrow x\lambda Ry\lambda \quad (\lambda \geqq 0).$$

Given any demand $(x, p) \in \Omega^n \times \Omega_n$ and utility relation $R \subset \Omega^n \times \Omega^n$, $H(R; x, p)$ is the assertion that R is an order (reflexive and transitive) compatible with the demand by the conditions

$$py \leqq px \Rightarrow xRy, \quad yRx \Rightarrow py \geqq px.$$

From the definition of H,

$$H(R; x, p) \Rightarrow H(R; x, \lambda p) \quad (\lambda \geqq 0).$$

Then with

$$E(R; p) = [x : H(R; x, p)]$$

defining the *expansion locus* of R for prices p, that is the locus of bundles x the demand of which at prices p is compatible with R, there is the property

$$E(R; p) = E(R; \lambda p) \quad (\lambda > 0).$$

Thus the expansion locus depends only on the ray

$$\vec{p} = [\lambda p : \lambda \geqq 0]$$

through p, and the same locus is obtained when p is replaced by any other point on the ray except 0. The *demand system* associated with R is

$$F(R; p, M) = [x : H(R; x, p), \quad px = M]$$

$$= [x : x \in E(R; p), \quad px = M],$$

and it has properties

$$x \in F(R; p, M) \Rightarrow px = M,$$

$$F(R; p, M) = F(R; \lambda p, \lambda M) \quad (\lambda > 0).$$

The effect of imposing the conical restriction on R is to obtain the property

$$H(R; x, p) \Rightarrow H(R; x\lambda, p) \quad (\lambda > 0),$$

not valid without it. Another statement is that the expansion loci $E(R; p)$ are conical, that is

$$x \in E(R; p) \Rightarrow x\lambda \in E(R; p) \quad (\lambda > 0);$$

or for the demand system

$$F(R; p, \lambda M) = \lambda F(R; p, M),$$

equivalently

$$F(R; \lambda^{-1}p, M) = \lambda F(R; p, M).$$

2. *Homogeneous consistency*

Demands (x_t, p_t) $(t = 0, 1)$ being given, let $\dot{H}(R)$ be the assertion that R is a utility order with which they are simultaneously compatible and moreover that R is conical. Then $\dot{H}$ asserts the existence of such R, or *homogeneous consistency* of the demands.

Let

$$\sigma_{rs} = p_r x_s / p_r x_r = u_r x_s$$

so $\sigma_{rr} = 1$. The condition on the two demands given by

$$\dot{K} \equiv p_0 x_1 p_1 x_0 \geqq p_0 x_0 p_1 x_1$$

is then the same as

$$\sigma_{01} \sigma_{01} \geqq 1.$$

A condition on any numbers $\phi = (\phi_0, \phi_1)$ is given by

$$\dot{S}(\phi) \equiv \phi_t > 0, \quad \sigma_{st} \geqq \phi_t / \phi_s$$

and let S assert the existence of such ϕ.

For any ϕ_t $(t = 0, 1)$ let

$$\phi_t(x) = \phi_t p_t x / p_t x_t = \phi_t u_t x,$$

and let

$$\phi(x) = \min \phi_t(x).$$

Then let $\dot{C}(\phi)$ assert simultaneous compatibility of the demands with the classical homogeneous utility represented by the function $\phi(x)$ thus constructed from $\phi = (\phi_0, \phi_1)$. Let $\dot{C}$ assert the existence of such ϕ, so immediately $\dot{C} \Rightarrow \dot{H}$.

These conditions $\dot{H}$, $\dot{K}$, $\dot{S}$ and $\dot{C}$ can readily be seen to be restrictions of the earlier defined H, K, S and C.

$$\dot{H} \Rightarrow H$$

$$\dot{K} \Rightarrow K$$

$$\dot{S}(\phi) \iff S(\phi, \phi), \quad \text{so} \quad \dot{S} \Rightarrow S$$

$$\dot{C}(\phi) \iff C(\phi, \phi), \quad \text{so} \quad \dot{C} \Rightarrow C.$$

Just as the earlier ones were proved equivalent, the same will appear for these.

THEOREM 2.1 $\dot{H} \Rightarrow \dot{K}$.

Suppose $\dot{H}(R)$, that is

$$u_t x \leqq 1 \Rightarrow x_t Rx, \quad xRx_t \Rightarrow u_t x \geqq 1$$

for conical R. Then for $x = x_s t_s$ such that $u_t x_s t_s = 1$ it follows that $x_t Rx_s t_s$, equivalently $x_t t_s^{-1} Rx_s$ since R is conical, that is $x_t u_t x_s Rx_s$. Similarly $x_s Rx_t (u_s x_t)^{-1}$. Hence, by transitivity of R,

$$x_t u_t x_s Rx_t (u_s x_t)^{-1},$$

equivalently

$$x_t (u_t x_s)(u_s x_t) Rx_t.$$

But by $\dot{H}(R)$ this implies

$$u_t x_t (u_t x_s)(u_s x_t) \geqq 1.$$

But $u_t x_t = 1$, so this gives

$$u_t x_s u_s x_t \geqq 1,$$

that is $\dot{K}$.

THEOREM 2.2 $\dot{K} \Rightarrow \dot{S}$.

Suppose $\dot{K}$, that is

$$u_0 x_1 u_1 x_0 \geqq 1.$$

Then

$$u_0 x_1 \geqq 1/u_1 x_0,$$

so there exists ϕ_1 such that

$$u_0 x_1 \geqq \phi_1 \geqq 1/u_1 x_0.$$

This with $\phi_0 = 1$ gives ϕ $(t = 0, 1)$ such that

$$u_s x_t \geqq \phi_t / \phi_s,$$

that is $\dot{S}(\phi)$, demonstrating $\dot{S}$.

THEOREM 2.3 $\dot{S}(\phi) \Rightarrow \dot{C}(\phi)$.

For any ϕ_t let

$$\phi_t(x) = \phi_t u_t x,$$

and

$$\phi(x) = \min_{t} \phi_t(x),$$

so for all t

$$\phi(x) \leqq \phi_t(x)$$

and

$$\phi(x) = \phi_t(x) \quad <=> \quad \phi_t(x) \leqq \phi_s(x) \quad \text{for all} \quad s.$$

Also

$$\phi_t(x_t) = \phi_t,$$

and so if $\phi_t > 0$

$$u_t x < 1 \Rightarrow \phi(x) \leqq \phi_t(x) < \phi_t$$

$$\Rightarrow \phi(x) < \phi_t.$$

Now if $\dot{S}(\phi)$, then

$$\phi_t(x_t) = \phi_t \leqq \phi_s u_s x_t = \phi_s(x_t),$$

and also

$$u_t x \leqq 1 \Rightarrow \phi(x) \leqq \phi_t,$$

and hence

$$\phi(x_t) = \phi_t.$$

Then also, since $\phi_t > 0$

$$u_t x < 1 \Rightarrow \phi(x) < \phi(x_t)$$

$$u_t x \leqq 1 \Rightarrow \phi(x) \leqq \phi(x_t).$$

This shows the utility is simultaneously compatible with the demands, that is $\dot{C}(\phi)$, as required.

COROLLARY $\dot{S} \Rightarrow \dot{C}$.

THEOREM 2.4 $\dot{H} \iff \dot{K} \iff \dot{S} \iff \dot{C}$.

The previous theorems give

$$\dot{H} \Rightarrow \dot{K} \Rightarrow \dot{S} \Rightarrow \dot{C}.$$

But it is immediate from the definitions that $\dot{C} \Rightarrow \dot{H}$.

3. *Revealed homogeneous preference*

The revealed preference relation of demand t has been defined as

$$R_t = (x_t, Wu_t)$$
$$= [(x_t, x) : u_t x \leqq 1].$$

Now define the *revealed homogeneous preference relation* as the conical closure of this, that is

$$\dot{R}_t = [R_t \rho : \rho \geqq 0]$$
$$= [(x_t \rho, x\rho) : u_t x\rho \leqq \rho, \rho \geqq 0]$$
$$= [(x_t \rho, x) : u_t x \leqq \rho]$$

it being understood that $x \geqq 0$. Thus

$$\dot{R}_t = [(x_t \rho, x) : u_t x \leqq \rho].$$

From this definition, $\dot{R}_t$ is conical and

$$R_t \subset \dot{R}_t.$$

For the cost-efficiency condition, required by compatability between demand t and a utility R,

$$H_t^!(R) \quad <=> \quad R_t \subset R.$$

Taking conical closures

$$R_t \subset R => \dot{R}_t \subset \dot{R}.$$

But if R is conical, so $\dot{R} = R$, since in any case $R_t \subset \dot{R}_t$, it follows that

$$\dot{R}_t \subset \dot{R} => R_t \subset \dot{R}_t \subset R.$$

Thus, with conical R

$$R_t \subset R \quad <=> \quad \dot{R}_t \subset \dot{R}.$$

Consequently,

$$\dot{H}_t^!(R) \quad <=> \quad \dot{R}_t \subset R,$$

since $\dot{H}$ is H joined with the assertion that R is conical.

The revealed homogeneous preference relation of several demands is defined as the transitive closure of the union of their individual revealed homogeneous preference relations. Thus for the two given demands, their revealed homogeneous preference relation is

$$\dot{R}_{01} = \dot{R}_0 \overset{\rightarrow}{\cup} \dot{R}_1.$$

It is conical, and has the property

$$\dot{H}'(R) \quad <=> \quad \dot{R}_{01} \subset R.$$

With this it will be seen later that, besides

$$\dot{H}(R) => \dot{R}_{01} \subset R,$$

also

$$\dot{H} \quad <=> \quad \dot{H}(\dot{R}_{01}),$$

and these properties justify the definition of $\dot{R}_{01}$.

From the definition of $\dot{R}_t$,

$$x\dot{R}_t y \quad <=> \quad (\forall t, \rho)x = x_t \rho, \quad u_t y \leqq \rho.$$

Then from the definition of $\dot{R}_{01}$, the cases of elements which have this relation are

$$x_0 \rho \dot{R}_{01} x_0 \sigma \quad <=> \quad (\forall m)(u_0 x_1 u_1 x_0)^m \leqq \rho/\sigma,$$

and

$$x_0 \rho \dot{R}_{01} x_1 \sigma \quad <=> \quad (\forall m)(u_0 x_1 u_1 x_0)^m u_0 x_1 \leqq \rho/\sigma.$$

Further

$$x_0 \rho \dot{R}_{01} x \quad <=> \quad (\forall t, \sigma)x_0 \rho \dot{R}_{01} x_t \sigma, \quad u_t x \leqq \sigma.$$

Then to complete the description of $\dot{R}_{01}$,

$$x\dot{R}_{01} y \quad <=> \quad (\forall t, \rho)x = x_t \rho, \quad x_t \rho \dot{R}_{01} y.$$

THEOREM 3.1 $\dot{K} \quad <=> \quad \dot{R}_{01} \subset \overline{\mathcal{E}}.$

Suppose

$$x\dot{R}_{01}y, \quad x < y$$

for some x, y or, equivalently,

$$x_t \rho \dot{R}_{01} y, \quad x_t \rho < y$$

for some t, ρ and y, or again

$$x_t \rho \dot{R}_{01} x_s \sigma, \quad u_s y \leq \sigma, \quad x_t \rho < y$$

for some s, t, ρ, σ and y. If $s = t$ this is equivalent to

$$x_t \rho \dot{R}_{01} x_t \sigma, \quad \rho < \sigma$$

which implies

$$(\vee m)(u_0 x_1 u_1 x_0)^m \leq \rho/\sigma < 1$$

which is impossible unless

$$u_0 x_1 u_1 x_0 < 1,$$

contradicting $\dot{K}$. In the case $s \neq t$, instead there is equivalence to

$$x_t \rho \dot{R}_{01} x_s \sigma, \quad u_s x_t \rho < \sigma,$$

which implies

$$(\vee m)(u_0 x_1 u_1 x_0)^m u_t x_s \leq \rho/\sigma < 1/u_s x_t,$$

which again implies the contradiction of $\dot{K}$. This proves half the theorem. To prove the converse, now suppose $u_0 x_1 u_1 x_0 < 1$, this being the denial of $\dot{K}$. Then

$$x_0 \dot{R}_{01} x_1 \sigma$$

where $\sigma = (u_0 x_1 u_1 x_0)^{-1} > 1$. Then since $u_0 x_0 = 1 < \sigma$, there exists $x > x_0$ such that $u_0 x \leq \sigma$. But then $x_0 \dot{R}_{01} x$, giving a contradiction of $\dot{R}_{01} \subset \overline{\oslash}$. The theorem is now proved.

THEOREM 3.2 $\dot{H} \iff \dot{H}(\dot{R}_{01})$.

It suffices to see that

$$\dot{K} \iff x_s \rho \dot{R}_{01} x_t \implies u_t x_s \rho \geq 1.$$

But this follows from

$$x_s \rho \dot{R}_{01} x_t \quad \Longleftrightarrow \quad (\vee m)(u_0 x_1 u_1 x_0)^m u_s x_t \leqq \rho$$

$$x_s \rho \dot{R}_{01} x_s \quad \Longleftrightarrow \quad (\vee m)(u_0 x_1 u_1 x_0)^m \leqq \rho.$$

4. *Range of the price index*

Consider any R such that $\dot{H}(R)$, so R is conical and simultaneously compatible with the demands (x_t, p_t). It is compatible also with any demand $(x_t\lambda, p_t)$ for $\lambda \geqq 0$. The point $x_t\lambda$ on the ray through x_t corresponds to an income $M_t = p_t x_t \lambda$, so $x_t M_t / p_t x_t$ corresponds to the income M_t. Then the equivalent income at prices s is

$$M_s = \inf[p_s x : xRx_t M_t / p_t x_t]$$

$$= \frac{M_t}{p_t x_t} \inf[p_s x : xRx_t].$$

Thus

$$M_s / M_t = P_{st}(R)$$

where

$$P_{st}(R) = \frac{1}{p_t x_t} \inf[p_s x : xRx_t]$$

$$= \frac{p_s x_s}{p_t x_t} \inf[u_s x : xRx_t].$$

This is the price index between the periods as determined by the homogeneous utility R simultaneously compatible with the demands in them. It is required to determine its range for all complete and non-satiated such R. It is convenient to do this in terms of the critical cost functions, which in application to a conical relation will be denoted $\hat{\Pi}$, $\check{\Pi}$ and which for these R coincide in the function

$$\Pi_{st}(R) = \inf[u_s x : xRx_t],$$

from which the price index is determined as

$$P_{st}(R) = \frac{p_s x_s}{p_t x_t} \Pi_{st}(R).$$

The values

$$\hat{\Pi}_{st} = \hat{\Pi}_{st}(\dot{R}_{01}), \quad \check{\Pi}_{st} = \check{\Pi}_{st}(\dot{R}_{01})$$

when R is the revealed homogeneous preference relation $\dot{R}_{01}$ will be determined under the hypothesis $\dot{K}$. Since

$$\dot{K} \iff \dot{H} \iff \dot{H}(\dot{R}_{10})$$

and

$$\dot{H}(R) \implies \dot{R}_{01} \subset R,$$

it will follow, for R which is complete and non-satiated, so $\hat{\Pi}$, $\check{\Pi}$ coincide in Π, that

$$\dot{H}(R) \implies \check{\Pi}_{rs} \leqq \Pi_{rs}(R) \leqq \hat{\Pi}_{rs}.$$

5. Revealed bounds

THEOREM 5.1 $\dot{K}$ <=> $\hat{\Pi}_{rs} = u_r x_s$, $\overline{\dot{K}}$ <=> $\hat{\Pi}_{rs} = 0$.

Thus,

$$\hat{\Pi}_{rs} = \inf\lceil u_r x : x\dot{R}_{01}x_s \rceil$$
$$= \inf[u_r x_t \rho : x_t \rho \dot{R}_{01} x_s]$$
$$= u_r x_s \inf[\rho : (\vee m)(u_0 x_1 u_1 x_0)^m \leq \rho]$$
$$= u_r x_s \quad \text{if} \quad u_0 x_1 u_1 x_0 \geq 0,$$

and otherwise the value is 0.

THEOREM 5.2 $\dot{K}$ <=> $\check{\Pi}_{rs} = 1/u_s x_r$, $\overline{\dot{K}}$ <=> $\check{\Pi}_{rs} = \infty$.

Thus,

$$\check{\Pi}_{rs} = \inf\lceil u_r x : x_s \overline{\dot{R}}_{01} x \rceil$$
$$= \inf\lceil u_r x : x_s \dot{R}_{01} x_t \rho => u_t x \geq \rho \rceil.$$

But

$$x_s \dot{R}_{01} x_s \rho \quad <=> \quad (\vee m)(u_0 x_1 u_1 x_0)^m \leq 1/\rho$$
$$x_s \dot{R}_{01} x_r \rho \quad <=> \quad (\vee m)(u_0 x_1 u_1 x_0)^m u_s x_r \leq 1/\rho$$

showing that if $\dot{K}$ does not hold then the value is ∞, and otherwise

$$\check{\Pi}_{rs} = \inf\lceil u_r x : u_s x \geq 1, \quad u_r x \geq 1/u_s x_r \rceil.$$

From here immediately

$$\check{\Pi}_{rs} \geq 1/u_s x_r.$$

But also $x = x_r/u_s x_r$ is a feasible solution, showing that

$$\check{\Pi}_{rs} = u_r x = u_r x_r/u_s x_r = 1/u_s x_r.$$

THEOREM 5.3   For complete nonsatiated R,

$$\dot{H}(R) => 1/u_s x_r \leq \Pi_{rs}(R) \leq u_r x_s.$$

This follows from Theorems 5.1 and 5.2 together with the remarks at the end of the last section.

6. *Classical limits*

It is to be shown now that, even under further restriction on R that it be classical, the bounds shown in Theorem 5.3 are attained, so they are in fact limits, and also every value between these limits is attained.

THEOREM 6.1   For ϕ_t *such that*

$$\phi_t > 0, \quad u_s x_t \geq \phi_t/\phi_s$$

and

$$\phi_t(x) = \phi_t u_t x, \quad \phi(x) = \min_t \phi_t(x),$$

the range of

$$\Pi_{rs}(\phi) = \min[u_r x : \phi(x) \geq \phi(x_s)]$$

is the closed interval with upper and lower limits $u_r x_s$, $1/u_s x_r$.

The conditions on ϕ_t assure that

$$\phi_s(x_s) = \phi_s \leq \phi_t u_t x_s = \phi_t(x_s),$$

so that

$$\phi(x_s) = \min[\phi_s(x_s), \quad \phi_t(x_s)]$$

$$= \phi_s(x_s)$$

$$= \phi_t.$$

Hence

$$\Pi_{rs}(\phi) = \min[u_r x : \phi(x) \geq \phi_s]$$

$$= \min[u_r x : \phi_s(x) \geq \phi_s, \quad \phi_r(x) \geq \phi_s]$$

$$= \min[u_r x : u_s x \geq 1, \quad u_r x \geq \phi_s/\phi_r].$$

But if any such ϕ_t exist at all, for which the condition is $\dot{K}$, that is $u_r x_s u_s x_r \geq 1$, then also it is possible to take

$$u_r x_s \geq \phi_s/\phi_r \geq 1/u_s x_r$$

where

$$\phi_s/\phi_r = \theta/u_s x_r + (1 - \theta)u_r x_s$$

for $0 \leqq \theta \leqq 1$. Then

$$\Pi_{rs}(\phi) = \min[u_r x : u_s x \geqq 1, \ u_r x \geqq \theta/u_s x_r + (1 - \theta)u_r x_s].$$

From this immediately

$$\Pi_{rs}(\phi) \geqq \theta/u_s x_r + (1 - \theta)u_r x_s.$$

But also

$$x = x_r \theta/u_s x_r + x_s(1 - \theta)$$

is feasible and gives

$$u_r x = \theta/u_s x_r + (1 - \theta)u_r x_s,$$

showing that

$$\Pi_{rs}(\phi) = \theta/u_s x_r + (1 - \theta)u_r x_s.$$

This establishes that $\Pi_{rs}(\phi)$ takes the values $u_r x_s$ and $1/u_s x_r$, and every intermediate value.

Since the condition which the $\phi = (\phi_0, \phi_1)$ are subject to is $S(\phi)$, and this implies the condition $C(\phi)$ that the polyhedral classical function $\phi(x)$ constructed from them represents a relation R such that $\dot{H}(R)$, there is the following.

THEOREM 6.2   *The range of* $\Pi_{rs}(R)$ *for all complete non-satiated* R *such that* $\dot{H}(R)$ *is the closed interval with upper and lower limits*

$u_r x_s$ *and* $1/u_s x_r$.

The proof follows from the last two theorems, together with the remarks made at the beginning of the section.

COROLLARY   *The range of*

$$P_{rs} = \inf[p_r x : xR x_s]$$

for all complete non-satiated R *such that* $\dot{H}(R)$ *is the closed interval with upper and lower limits given by the Laspeyres and Paasche indices*

$$\hat{p}_{rs} = p_r x_s/p_s x_s, \quad \overset{\vee}{p}_{rs} = p_r x_r/p_s x_r.$$

IV : FISHER AND QUADRATICS

Introduction

For any pair of demands, a necessary and sufficient
condition for the existence of a compatible homogeneous utility, and
hence of a compatible (or "true") price index, is the PL-*inequality,*
which is that the Paasche index does not exceed that of Laspeyres.
This is the condition for the PL-*interval,* or the set of points bounded
above and below by the Laspeyres and Paasche indices, to be non-empty.
A *compatible price index* being one determined in respect to some
compatible homogeneous utility, its possible values are identical with
the points of the PL-interval. When the interval is non-empty, the
Fisher "ideal" index is one of its points and therefore has this
property of compatibility like any other. There are results coming
directly from the last chapter.

Thus, whenever there exists *any* value at all which can be
established as a price index on the basis of utility, the Fisher index
provides *one* such value. But then *so also do all the points in the*
PL-*interval,* these being the Paasche and Laspeyres indices themselves
together with every value between them. The Fisher index therefore is
not uniquely distinguished by being derivable on the basis of utility,
since it shares the distinction with all the points of the PL-interval.
Also it has that distinction at all only when that interval is non-empty,
which is to say when the PL-inequality holds.

Buscheguennce (1925) seemed to offer a special distinction
for the Fisher index; at least, he showed what appeared to be a possible
route leading towards this. But though the route was established it was

never travelled. The conclusion that the Fisher index is derivable on
the basis of utility requires the existence of a quadratic utility
compatible with the given demands, and this starting position was not
even approached. Buscheguennce showed that if there were a compatible
homogeneous quadratic utility then the Fisher index would correspond to
it. At the time a primary significance — which, with the foregoing
results, has now evaporated — could have been that it seemed the "ideal"
formula could become distinguished among the great variety of index
formulae as being directly derivable on the basis of utility, making
it more ideal than ever. That a specifically quadratic utility is
involved then would have been a secondary part of the matter, though
this is now the interest which remains. It had only seemed the index
might be thus derivable because there was no notice that the hypothesis
required might be impossible. The neglect does not diminish the nicety
of the result that if such a quadratic exists there is no need to
actually identify it to find the index which derives from it: all that
needs to be known is computed by the Fisher formula from the pair of
demands with which it is required to be compatible. But still the
existence question remains; it is not completely straightforward ...

That a homogeneous quadratic could be compatible with given
demands is certainly true. We are quite accustomed to illustrating
by the example with rectangular hyperbolae $x_1 x_2 = k$. This example falls
under cases of both quadratic and Cobb-Douglas utility. It is safest
to regard it as falling under the latter: any Cobb-Douglas looks like
a good utility function, but not any quadratic. Here is a hint of the
syndrome of unpleasantness in the quadratic existence question taken as

it stands. But it will not be taken as it stands.

For the existence of any compatible homogeneous utility, the PL-inequality is necessary and sufficient. But required now is the existence of a utility with a restriction in addition to homogeneity. For this the PL-inequality must be necessary, but a sufficient condition could have to be stronger. If the additional restriction on utility is that it be quadratic, any sufficient condition does indeed have to be stronger, and it is in a way which is entirely without "economic" significance or interest. Inspection shows this, and without an independent impulse for the chore there is no sense to investigate such a condition. However, a simple change in the quadratic requirement abolishes any unwanted intricacies.

Rather than asking for a utility which is quadratic, that is representable by a quadratic function, instead let the requirement be weaker and ask for a utility which is *locally quadratic* in the sense that it has a quadratic representation at least in some neighbourhood containing the demand points x_0, x_1. With this definition there is a simple result: *the PL-inequality is both necessary and sufficient for the existence of a compatible locally quadratic utility.*

Buscheguennce's theorem remains true, and is enlarged, when the quadratic utility is replaced by one which is only locally quadratic. So now there is the theorem which enlarges this enlargement of it: for any pair of demands, *whenever compatible price indices exist, the Fisher index is one, and is distinguished as corresponding to a locally quadratic utility.*

A descendant of Buscheguennce's theorem, which inherits all

its defects and adds to them from a more ample opportunity, is the

"New Formula" of Wald (1939). Another relative is a formula of Afriat

(1956) (referred to elsewhere here, and reproduced in Shubik (1968)),

also not without a defect, which can still be remedied. But Wald's

formula is so immediate a relative as to be a corollary.

Wald remarked that the expansion loci of a quadratic utility

are lines. In fact, they break into linear parts which generally lie

in linear manifolds. They lie in lines only when the quadratic is

regular, having a unique centre, where the gradient vanishes and where

the expansion lines are all concurrent, and are terminated — they cannot

be complete lines but at most half lines, or segments where the half

lines cut the commodity space.

Wald took a pair of expansion lines L_0, L_1 and associated

prices p_0, p_1 to be given, and considered the hypothesis that they

belonged to a quadratic utility. But if the lines are meant to contain

complete expansion loci of a quadratic, the quadratic must be regular,

and hence, for consistency with the hypothesis, the lines must intersect.

Let c be their intersection, so with this the lines are specified by any

other points x_0, x_1 on them. Then the quadratic in x becomes a homo-

geneous quadratic in $z = x-c$, when the origin in the commodity space is

changed to c. Also, a budget constraint $p_0 x = M_0$ is equivalent to

$p_0(x-c) = M_0 - p_0 c_0$, and becomes $p_0 z = N_0$ with the change of origin, where

$N_0 = M_0 - p_0 c_0$; the point x_0 on L_0 corresponds to $d_0 = x_0 - c_0$; the line L_0

becomes the ray through d_0; and similarly with 1 in place of 0.

Now to establish the equivalence of incomes M_0, M_1 with the

general quadratic, it is as if incomes N_0, N_1 were to be equivalent for a homogeneous quadratic which is compatible with demands (d_0, p_0), (d_1, p_1). For this equivalence, Buscheguennce's theorem applies to give the condition

$$N_1 = P_{10}N_0,$$

where

(i) $$P_{10} = (p_1 d_0 p_1 d_1 / p_0 d_0 p_0 d_1)^{\frac{1}{2}}$$

Thus the relation between equivalent incomes M_0, M_1 is

(ii) $$M_1 - E_1 = P_{10}(M_0 - E_0)$$

where

(iii) $$E_0 = p_0 c, \; E_1 = p_1 c.$$

are the *income origins*. This therefore must be what Wald's "New Formula" asserts, in the case where the hypothesis is for a regular quadratic utility.

A similar, though more intricate argument applies to the case where the lines L_0, L_1 do not intersect, though now the hypothetical quadratic cannot be regular, and the lines cannot contain complete expansion loci of it, since these must be of higher dimension.

The lines generally have no common point c. Instead *critical points* c_0, c_1 are determined on them such that

(iv) $$p_0 c_0 = p_0 c_1, \quad p_1 c_0 = p_1 c_1.$$

These exist and are unique provided

(v) $$\begin{vmatrix} p_0 d_0 & p_0 d_1 \\ p_1 d_0 & p_1 d_1 \end{vmatrix} \neq 0$$

Income origins are now determined from

(vi) $E_0 = p_0 c_0, \quad E_1 = p_1 c_1$

Just as well, giving the same values, they could be determined as before
with a point c no longer the intersection of the lines, which no longer
generally exists, but instead any point on the *critical transversal* T
which is the join of c_0, c_1. This preserves precisely the form of the
first derived formula. Should the lines intersect, the critical points
coincide in their intersection, the critical transversal degenerates to
this point, and the first formula is recovered from the second.

As formulae, these are nowhere visible in the dense algebra
which makes the "New Formula" of Wald. They should coincide with his
simply because they have the same premise and are directed to the same
question and so, hopefully, give the same answer.

The relation (ii) between incomes M_0, M_1 which, as decided
by the hypothetical quadratic, have the same purchasing power at prices
p_0, p_1 is a general linear relation, with slope P_{10} given by (i) and
defining the *incremental price index*. It shows a departure from the
price-index idea, which requires a homogeneous linear relation.

Should the lines L_0, L_1 be rays, that is lines through the
origin, then

(vii) $c_0 = c_1 = 0$

so

(viii) $E_0 = E_1 = 0 \quad$ and $\quad d_0 = x_0, d_1 = x_1,$

and hence the equivalent income relation (ii) reduces to the homogeneous
linear relation

(ix) $M_1 = P_{10} M_0,$

where

$$(x) \qquad P_{10} = (p_1 x_0 p_1 x_1 / p_0 x_0 p_0 x_1)^{\frac{1}{2}},$$

this being the Fisher price index, a function of the rays through the points x_0, x_1 rather than of the points themselves, these being arbitrary points on the lines L_0, L_1 which in the present case are rays.

The introduction of the critical points not only enables the statement, and the derivation, of Wald's formula to be simplified. It also gives the terms required in a criterion for the applicability of the "New Formula" and, generally, of any formula for purchasing power comparison between incomes M_0, M_1 on the basis of the given data. This applicability criterion first makes a distinction between *hyperbolic* and *elliptical cases*, by the conditions

$$p_0 d_0 p_1 d_1 < p_1 d_0 p_0 d_1 \quad \text{and} \quad p_0 d_0 p_1 d_1 > p_1 d_0 p_0 d_1$$

Then incomes M_0, $M_1 > 0$ which are comparable in the hyperbolic case must satisfy $M_0 \geqq E_0$, $M_1 \geqq E_1$, and those which are so in the elliptical case must satisfy $M_0 \leqq E_0$, $M_1 \geqq E_1$. It appears from here that there can be no entertainment of quite arbitrary comparisons between incomes, but the ranges of incomes to enter into comparisons must be made specific in advance and then it can be decided whether they are permissible or not. Emphasizing this, there are instances where no incomes can enter into comparison at all, such as in the elliptical case with E_0, $E_1 \leqq 0$. With homogeneity, when $E_0 = E_1 = 0$, only in the hyperbolic case are any incomes comparable. The hyperbolic condition then reduces to $p_0 x_0 p_1 x_1 < p_0 x_1 p_1 x_0$, which is simply the requirement that the Paasche index does not exceed that of Laspeyres. Here therefore is a further perspective on that already familiar requirement.

FIGURE 14

Critical Points and the Incremental Price Index

(p_0, L_0), (p_1, L_1) the given linear expansions

c_0, c_1 the critical points lying on L_0, L_1

such that $p_0 c_0 = p_0 c_1$, $p_1 c_0 = p_1 c_1$

T the critical transversal, their join

$E_0 = p_0 c$, $E_1 = p_1 c$ the critical incomes

fixed for all c on T

x_0, x_1 any other points on L_0, L_1

$d_0 = x_0 - c_0$, $d_1 = x_1 - c_1$ "incremental bundles"

specifying the directions of L_0, L_1

$\hat{P}_{10} = p_1 d_0 / p_0 d_0$, $\check{P}_1 = p_1 d_1 / p_0 d_1$, $\bar{P}_{10} = (\hat{P}_{10} \check{P}_{10})^{\frac{1}{2}}$

incremental price indices

the "incremental" counterparts of the

Laspeyres, Paasche and Fisher price indices

Income Purchasing Power

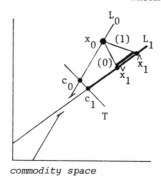

commodity space

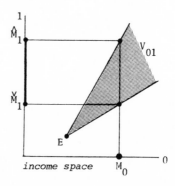

income space

incomes M_0, M_1 which are

equivalent in purchasing power

as decided by any utility order

compatible with the given linear expansions

are in a correspondence $M_1 - E_1 = P_{10} (M_0 - E_0)$

the incremental price index P_{10} being

indeterminate in the interval $\overset{\vee}{P}_{10} \leqq P_{10} \leqq \hat{P}_{10}$

Wald's "New Formula"

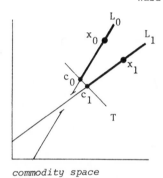

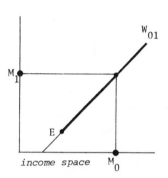

commodity space   income space M_0

Wald's "New Formula" is simply $P_{10} = \overline{P}_{10}$

Hyperbolic and Elliptical Cases

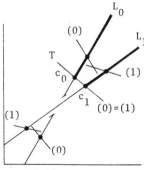

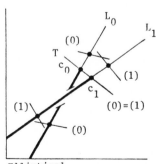

Hyperbolic
$$p_0 d_1 p_1 d_0 > p_0 d_0 p_1 d_1$$

Elliptical
$$p_0 d_1 p_1 d_0 < p_0 d_0 p_1 d_1$$

for compatibility with any utility order

the expansion lines must be truncated to

half-lines with the critical points as vertices

which halves are admitted being decided by

the case being hyperbolic or elliptical

$$p_0 d_0 p_1 d_1 \; < \; \text{or} \; > \; p_0 d_1 p_1 d_0$$

consequently only restricted ranges of incomes M_0, M_1

can enter into purchasing power correspondence at all

in the hyperbolic case those with $M_0 \geqq E_0$, $M_1 \geqq E_1$

and in the elliptical case those with $M_0 \leqq E_0$, $M_1 \leqq E_1$.

omitted in this description is the non-central or

parabolic case $p_0 d_0 p_1 d_1 = p_0 d_1 p_1 d_0$

(see Afriat, Karlsruhe Seminar, 1976)

the illustrations here show the hyperbolic case with E_0, $E_1 > 0$

1. Buscheguennce on Fisher

Robin Marris made a remark (see **Preface**) to the effect that Buscheguennce (1925) showed Fisher's index to be "exact" if utility is a homogeneous quadratic. Without having seen it, the following seems a likely content of the paper, based on the remark.

A homogeneous quadratic has the form

$$\phi(x) = \tfrac{1}{2} x'hx,$$

where h is a symmetric matrix, the Hessian of the function. The gradient is then

$$g(x) = x'h.$$

It has the property

$$g(x_0)x_1 = x_0'hx_1$$
$$= x_1'hx_0$$
$$= g(x_1)x_0,$$

since $h = h'$. Also

$$\phi(x) = \tfrac{1}{2}g(x)x.$$

THEOREM 1.1   *If* (x_0, p_0), (x_1, p_1) *are a pair of demands which are simultaneously compatible with a homogeneous quadratic utility* $\phi(x)$ *then*

$$\phi(x_0) = \phi(x_1) \Rightarrow p_0x_0p_1x_0/p_0x_1p_1x_1 = 1$$

provided $x_0, x_1 > 0$.

Compatibility of $\phi(x)$ with (x_t, p_t) requires x_t to be a maximum of $\phi(x)$ subject to $p_tx = p_tx_t$, $x \geq 0$, and for this, with $x_t > 0$, it is necessary that

$$g(x_t) = \lambda_t p_t.$$

Compatibility also requires

$$p_t x < p_t x_t \Rightarrow \phi(x) < \phi(x_t)$$

and this implies $\lambda_t > 0$. Then

$$\lambda_0 p_0 x_1 = g(x_0) x_1$$
$$= g(x_1) x_0 = \lambda_1 p_1 x_0.$$

Also

$$\phi(x_t) = \tfrac{1}{2} g(x_t) x_t = \tfrac{1}{2} \lambda_t p_t x_t,$$

so $\phi(x_0) = \phi(x_1)$ is equivalent to

$$\lambda_0 p_0 x_0 = \lambda_1 p_1 x_1,$$

which with

$$\lambda_0 p_0 x_1 = \lambda_1 p_1 x_0$$

together with $\lambda_0, \lambda_1 \neq 0$ implies

$$p_0 x_0 / p_0 x_1 = p_1 x_1 / p_1 x_0.$$

COROLLARY (i)   *Under the same hypothesis, for any* $t_0, t_1 > 0$,

$$\phi(x_0 t_0) = \phi(x_1 t_1) \Rightarrow t_1^2 / t_0^2 = p_0 x_0 p_1 x_0 / p_0 x_1 p_1 x_1.$$

For if the demand (x_r, p_r), is compatible with a given homogeneous quadratic then so is the demand $(x_r t_r, p_r)$ for all $t_r > 0$, so the required conclusion follows just by replacing x_r by $x_r t_r$ in the conclusion of the theorem.

COROLLARY (ii)   *Under the same hypothesis, if incomes* M_0, M_1 *are determined by* $\phi(x)$ *to have the same purchasing power at prices* p_0, p_1 *then*

$$M_1 / M_0 = \overline{P}_{10}$$

where

$$\overline{P}_{10} = (p_1 x_0 p_1 x_1 / p_0 x_0 p_1 x_1)^{\frac{1}{2}},$$

this being Fisher's price index.

At prices p_r any income M_r purchases a bundle $x_r t_r$

where

$$p_r x_r t_r = M_r,$$

so

$$t_r = M_r/p_r x_r.$$

Then incomes M_0, M_1 have the same purchasing power at prices p_0, p_1

if $\phi(x_0 t_0) = \phi(x_1 t_1)$. By Corollary (i) this gives

$$(M_1 p_0 x_0/M_0 p_1 x_1)^2 = p_0 x_0 p_1 x_0/p_0 x_1 p_1 x_1,$$

as required.

The result about Fisher's index shown in Cor. (ii) is

understood to be Buscheguennce's Theorem.

2.   *Question about Buscheguennce*

The Theorem is true even if no quadratic exists to validate the hypothesis, but in that case it makes a vacuous comment on Fisher's index.   An interest arising from the theorem is therefore in the existence of such a quadratic.

The existence of a homogeneous quadratic utility simultaneously compatible with the demands can define their *homogeneous quadratic consistency*.   From the definition, this condition implies homogeneous consistency, which has been seen equivalent to the "Index Number Theorem" condition

$$\check{P}_{10} \leq \hat{P}_{10}$$

between the Laspeyres and Paasche indices, which implies that moreover

$$\check{P}_{10} \leq \overline{P}_{10} \leq \hat{P}_{10}.$$

Thus for homogeneous quadratic consistency, certainly the Laspeyres-Paasche test is necessary.   But since, at least on the surface, homogeneous quadratic consistency is more restrictive than homogeneous consistency, for which this test is necessary and sufficient, it would appear that this test is not sufficient.   Then it can be asked what additional test applied to the demands would give that sufficiency.

If the question is left as it is the answer is not simple. It is better to modify the question.   This can be done in a way which retains Buscheguennce's result, or rather amplifies it   by removing an inessential part of the hypothesis, and then the answer is simple, and possibly surprising: *no additional test is required*.

Let *local compatibility* between a demand   (x, p)   and a utility order   R   signify compatibility which has reference to some

neighbourhood of x instead of the entire commodity space. It requires
the usual conditions

$$py \leq px \Rightarrow xRy, \quad yRx \Rightarrow py \geq px$$

but for y near x, not for all $y \geq 0$. Everything in Theorem 1.1 and
Corollaries remains valid when compatibility is replaced by local compatibility, or alternatively when instead of a homogeneous quadratic
utility there is a homogeneous, or conical, utility relation R which
near the points x_t admits representation by a quadratic. There might
appear to be a difference between *homogeneous quadratic local consistency*
defined by simultaneous local compatibility with some homogeneous quadratic, and *local homogeneous quadratic consistency,* defined by simultaneous compatibility with some utility with the required homogeneous
quadratic local representation. But it appears there is none.

The proposed modification makes a difference because even
when there exist no compatible homogeneous quadratics there can exist
locally compatible homogeneous quadratics, signifying that though homogeneous quadratic consistency implies homogeneous quadratic local consistency the converse of this is not true.

While homogeneous quadratic local consistency readily implies
homogeneous consistency, there could well be the surmise that the converse
is not true, so there might be surprise that the converse is in fact true.

Reference to the more general problem with more than two
demands gives an explanation which reduces any surprise. In this problem
the converse, as can be guessed, is not true, but there is the theorem
that homogeneous quadratic local consistency is necessary and sufficient
homogeneous consistency together with the Fisher cyclical test applied

to the Fisher index

$$\overline{P}_{rs}\overline{P}_{st}\overline{P}_{tr} = 1.$$

The sufficiency part of this theorem is settled with some immediacy, and makes it sure that generally homogeneous consistency alone is not enough to give the required quadratic condition. But if there are just two demands this additional condition needed is automatically satisfied, since it reduces to the Fisher reversal test $\overline{P}_{10}\overline{P}_{01} = 1$ which is automatically satisfied by the Fisher index. From this follows the corollary that, with just two demands, homogeneous consistency is necessary and sufficient for homogeneous quadratic local consistency.

The outstanding feature of Buscheguennce's theorem on its own is that without even constructing a quadratic, or even knowing if a suitable one exists, all that would be relevant about it is obtained from the given pair of demands just by the Fisher index. The "New Formula" of Wald (1939) is a generalization, and Afriat (1956) gives a different generalization, which is also a generalization of Wald, as was pointed out by Houthakker with the cryptic statement (*circa* 1960) that twice two is four. When interpreted, this means that when the four demands used by Afriat have the price vectors equal in pairs and the corresponding pairs of quantity vectors are joined in lines the two linear expansions used by Wald are obtained. It can be verified that with this specialization of the prices Afriat's interval-indeterminacy formula reduces to Wald's point-determination formula, and it can be added, when these lines pass through the origin there is reduction of Wald's formula to Fisher's formula.

3. *Gradients and quadratics*

Simultaneous local compatibility of demands (x_0, p_0),

(x_1, p_1) and a utility $\phi(x)$ with gradient $g(x)$ requires

$$g_0 = \lambda_0 p_0, \quad g_1 = \lambda_1 p_1$$

for some $\lambda_0, \lambda_1 \neq 0$, where $g_0 = g(x_0)$, $g_1 = g(x_1)$. Then for $\phi(x)$

to be a homogeneous quadratic it is necessary that

$$g_0 x_1 = g_1 x_0,$$

that is

$$\lambda_0 p_0 x_1 = \lambda_1 p_1 x_0.$$

But given any pair of demands it is always possible to choose λ_0, λ_1

and to determine $g_0 = \lambda_0 p_0$, $g_1 = \lambda_1 p_1$ for which $g_0 x_1 = g_1 x_0$. It can

be asked then if there exists a homogeneous quadratic for which $g(x_0) =$

g_0, $g(x_1) = g_1$. It will appear now that this symmetry condition on the

gradients is sufficient to obtain that existence, and also that such

quadratics, though they then form an infinite variety, are essentially

unique in the linear space spanned by x_0, x_1.

THEOREM 3.1   *A necessary and sufficient condition that vectors* g_0, g_1

be the gradients of some homogeneous quadratic at points x_0, x_1 *is that*

$$\text{(i)} \qquad g_0 x_1 = g_1 x_0,$$

provided

$$\text{(ii)} \qquad \begin{vmatrix} g_0 x_0 & g_0 x_1 \\ g_1 x_0 & g_1 x_1 \end{vmatrix} \neq 0.$$

Then the values of all such quadratics at any point $x_0 \alpha_0 + x_1 \alpha_1$ *in the*

space spanned by x_0, x_1 *are the same, and equal to*

$$\text{(iii)} \qquad \tfrac{1}{2}(\alpha_0 g_0 + \alpha_1 g_1)(x_0 \alpha_0 + x_1 \alpha_1).$$

One such quadratic is

$$\text{(iv)} \qquad \Phi(x) = \tfrac{1}{2}x'Hx$$

where

$$H = G'(GX)^{-1}G$$

and

$$\text{(v)} \qquad X = (x_0, x_1), \quad G = \begin{pmatrix} g_0 \\ g_1 \end{pmatrix},$$

the matrix GX *being symmetric by (i) and regular by (ii). This quadratic has the property*

$$\text{(vi)} \qquad \Phi(x) = \Phi(ex)$$

where

$$\text{(vii)} \qquad e = X(GX)^{-1}G$$

is such that $e^2 = e$ *and is the projector onto the space* X *spanned by* x_0, x_1 *parallel to the orthogonal complement of the space* G *spanned by* g_0, g_1.

The necessity of (i) and the conclusion (iii) are immediate from general properties of a homogeneous quadratic.

The gradient of the quadratic $\Phi(x)$ given by (iv) is

$$G(x) = x'H.$$

It will be shown that

$$G(x_0) = g_0, \quad G(x_1) = g_1.$$

For any $\alpha = \begin{pmatrix} \alpha_0 \\ \alpha_1 \end{pmatrix}$, denote

$$x_\alpha = x_0\alpha_0 + x_1\alpha_1 = X\alpha,$$

$$g_\alpha = \alpha_0 g_0 + \alpha_1 g_1 = \alpha'G.$$

Then it suffices to show that

$$G(x_\alpha) = g_\alpha.$$

Thus, by (i) GX is symmetric, so

$$GX = (GX)' = X'G'.$$

and hence

$$G(x_\alpha) = x_\alpha' H$$
$$= \alpha' X' G' (GX)^{-1} G$$
$$= \alpha' GX (GX)^{-1} G$$
$$= \alpha' G$$
$$= g_\alpha,$$

as required.

It is immediate that e given by (vii) is idempotent, $e^2 = e$. Therefore it is the projector onto its range R_e parallel its null space N_e. But

$$R_e = [x : x = ey]$$
$$= [x : x = X(GX)^{-1}Gy]$$
$$= [x : x = Xz] = X.$$

Thus $R_e \subset X$. But also

$$eX = X(GX)^{-1}GX$$
$$= X,$$

which shows that $X \subset R_e$. Hence $R_e = X$. Also

$$N_e = [x : ex = 0]$$
$$= [x : x(GX)^{-1}Gx = 0]$$
$$\subset [x : Gx = 0] = \overline{G}$$

where $\overline{G}$ is the orthogonal complement of G. Thus $N_e \subset \overline{G}$. But R_e is of dimension 2, so N_e is of dimension $n - 2$, and $\overline{G}$ has the same dimension since G is of dimension 2. But a linear space has no proper subspaces of equal dimension, so it follows that $N_e = \overline{G}$.

Finally, with GX symmetric, it is verified directly that $e'He = H$ and from this (vi) follows.

4. Conditions for compatibility

For a utility function $\phi(x)$, with gradient $g(x)$, to be compatible with a demand (x, p) $(px > 0)$, the condition

$$g(x) = \lambda p, \quad \lambda > 0$$

is necessary, and if the function is quasiconcave this is also sufficient. Since $p \geq 0$, this condition requires $g(x) \geq 0$. If the function is $\phi(x) = \frac{1}{2}x'hx$, so $g(x) = x'h$ and $\phi(x) = \frac{1}{2}g(x)x$, the condition gives

$$2\phi(x) = \lambda px,$$

so also $\phi(x) > 0$.

There is no possibility of the function being established as quasiconcave by showing it concave. For the condition for ϕ to be concave is that the Hessian h be non-positive definite. But this means $\phi(x) \leq 0$ for all x, contradicting $\phi(x) > 0$. Also the possibility $\phi(x) \geq 0$ for all x is excluded, because this makes ϕ convex. Thus for ϕ to be quasiconcave in a region where it is positive it must necessarily be an indefinite quadratic form, taking both positive and negative values.

With $\phi(x) > 0$, it is possible to introduce $f(x) = (\phi(x))^{\frac{1}{2}}$, and this has the property

$$f(xt) = f(x)t.$$

A function with this property is quasiconcave if and only if it is concave. Thus ϕ is quasiconcave in a region where it is positive if and only if the Hessian of f is non-positive definite there.

The gradient of f is

$$G = \frac{1}{2}\phi^{-\frac{1}{2}}g$$

and the Hessian is

$$H = -\tfrac{1}{4}\phi^{-\frac{3}{2}}g'g + \tfrac{1}{2}\phi^{-\frac{1}{2}}h$$
$$= \tfrac{1}{2}\phi^{-\frac{3}{2}}(2\phi h - g'g).$$

Then, since

$$2\phi(x) = g(x)x, \quad g(y) = y'h$$

it follows that

$$y'H(x)y \leqq 0$$

if and only if

$$D(x, y) \leqq 0,$$

where

$$D(x, y) = g(x)x\, g(y)y - g(x)y\, g(y)x$$
$$= \begin{vmatrix} g(x)x & g(x)y \\ g(y)x & g(y)y \end{vmatrix}$$
$$= \begin{vmatrix} \begin{pmatrix} g(x) \\ g(y) \end{pmatrix} (x \ y) \end{vmatrix}.$$

With this condition, if it holds for a pair of points x, y
then it holds for every pair of points in the linear space spanned by
x, y. For let

$$z = x\lambda + y\mu, \quad z' = x\lambda' + y\mu'.$$

Then

$$D(z, z') = \Delta^2 D(x, y)$$

where

$$\Delta = \begin{vmatrix} \lambda & \lambda' \\ \mu & \mu' \end{vmatrix}.$$

Also, the value of ϕ at $z = x\lambda + y\mu$ is

$$\phi(z) = g(x)x\lambda^2 + 2g(x)y\lambda\mu + g(y)y\mu^2,$$

so $\phi(z) = 0$ for

$$\frac{\lambda}{\mu} = \frac{-g(x)y \pm \sqrt{-D(x,\, y)}}{g(x)x}.$$

If $D(x, y) < 0$, this determines two real values of λ/μ. Between these values $\phi(z)$ is positive and outside them it is negative, showing that the quadratic form is indefinite. In any case, if

$$\phi(x),\ \phi(y) > 0$$

and also

$$g(x)y = g(y)x \geqq 0$$

as is necessary if

$$g(x),\ g(y) \geq 0, \quad x,\ y \geq 0,$$

then

$$\phi(z) > 0 \quad \text{for} \quad (\lambda,\ \mu) \geqq 0.$$

These remarks lead to the following.

THEOREM 4.1   *For a homogeneous quadratic* ϕ *with gradient* g, *if*

$$x_0,\ x_1 \geqq 0,\quad g(x_0),\ g(x_1) \geq 0,\quad \phi(x_0),\ \phi(x_1) > 0$$

and

$$D(x_0,\ x_1) = g(x_0)x_0 g(x_1)x_1 - g(x_0)x_1 g(x_1)x_0 \neq 0,$$

then a necessary and sufficient condition for ϕ *to be quasiconcave in a convex neighbourhood of* $x_0,\ x_1$ *is that*

$$D(x_0,\ x_1) < 0.$$

For if this condition holds then $D(y_0, y_1) \leqq 0$ for all y_0, y_1 since it must hold for all $y_0,\ y_1$ near $x_0,\ x_1$ and therefore, as shown earlier, in the span of such $y_0,\ y_1$ and this span is the entire space. Also $\phi(x) > 0$ for $x \in \langle y_0, y_1 \rangle$ and $y_0,\ y_1$ near $x_0,\ x_1$ so there is a convex neighbourhood of $x_0,\ x_1$ where $\phi(x) > 0$. But $D(x, y) \leqq 0$ for x in this neighbourhood and all y, which, as already shown, assures ϕ is quasiconcave in this neighbourhood. Thus the condition is sufficient, and the necessity comes directly from the earlier remarks.

THEOREM 4.2   If

$$x_0, \; x_1 \geq 0, \quad g_0, \; g_1 \geq 0, \quad g_0 x_0, \; g_1 x_1 > 0,$$
$$g_0 x_1 = g_1 x_0,$$

and

$$g_0 x_0 g_1 x_1 \neq g_0 x_1 g_1 x_0,$$

so GX is regular, where

$$X = (x_0, \; x_1), \quad G = (g_0, \; g_1),$$

and if also

$$H = G'(GX)^{-1}G,$$

then a necessary and sufficient condition for the homogeneous quadratic

$$\Phi = \tfrac{1}{2}x'Hx$$

to be quasiconcave in a convex neighbourhood containing $x_0, \; x_1$ is that

$$g_0 x_0 g_1 x_1 < g_0 x_1 g_1 x_0.$$

For, by Theorem 3.1,

$$G(x_0) = g_0, \quad G(x_1) = g_1$$

so Theorem 4.1 gives the required conclusion.

Since only locally quadratic homogeneous utilities are being dealt with, there is need to consider their homogeneous, though not necessarily quadratic, extensions from a neighbourhood to the entire commodity space.

THEOREM 4.3   Any classical conical utility $\phi_0(x)$ $(x \in N_0)$ defined in a convex neighbourhood N_0 in the commodity space has a classical conical extension to the entire commodity space. There exists two such extensions $\overset{\vee}{\phi}(x)$, $\overset{\wedge}{\phi}(x)$ such that any function $\phi(x)$ is another if and only if it is *classical conical and*

$$\check{\phi}(x) \leqq \phi(x) \leqq \hat{\phi}(x)$$

for all x.

    Since ϕ_0 is conical it can be taken without loss in generality that N_0 is a convex cone. Then $\phi_0(x)$ is characterized by the convex set in N_0 given by

$$M_0 = [x : \phi_0(x) \geqq 1, \quad x \epsilon N_0],$$

since

$$\phi_0(x) = \max[t : \phi_0(x) \geqq t] \quad (x \epsilon N_0)$$

$$= \max[t : \phi_0(xt^{-1}) \geqq 1]$$

$$= \max[t : xt^{-1} \epsilon M_0].$$

    Let $\phi(x)$ be any homogeneous classical function that extends the definition of $\phi_0(x)$ to the entire commodity space. Then it determines the set

$$M = [x : \phi(x) \geqq 1, \quad x \epsilon \Omega^n],$$

from which it is recovered by the formula

$$\phi(x) = \max[t : xt^{-1} \epsilon M].$$

Then

$$\phi(x) = \phi_0(x) \quad (x \epsilon N_0),$$

if and only if

$$M_0 = M \cap N_0.$$

For $\phi(x)$ to be a classical function, M must be a closed orthoconvex set. It contains M_0 and has intersection M_0 with N_0 if and only if it lies between the set $\check{M}$ which is the orthoconvex closure of M_0, that is the smallest orthoconvex set containing M_0, and the largest orthoconvex set $\hat{M}$ whose intersection with N_0 does not exceed M_0. The functions $\check{\phi}, \hat{\phi}$ are defined by these sets.

5. *Theorem on quadratic consistency*

THEOREM 5.1   *For any demands* (x_0, p_0), (x_1, p_1) *such that*

$$p_0 x_0 p_1 x_1 \neq p_0 x_1 p_1 x_0,$$

a necessary and sufficient condition that there exists a homogeneous utility with which they are simultaneously compatible and which has a quadratic representation near x_0, x_1 *is that*

$$p_0 x_0 p_1 x_1 < p_0 x_1 p_1 x_0,$$

that is, the Laspeyres index is at least the Paasche index.

The necessity is already shown, since it has been shown that this is just the condition for homogeneous consistency, the existence of a compatible homogeneous utility, so it remains to prove the sufficiency.

Assuming the condition, so necessarily $p_0 x_1$, $p_1 x_0 > 0$, it is possible to choose λ_0, $\lambda_1 > 0$ so that

$$\lambda_0 p_0 x_1 = \lambda_1 p_1 x_0.$$

Then let

$$g_0 = \lambda_0 p_0, \quad g_1 = \lambda_1 p_1,$$
$$\phi_0 = \tfrac{1}{2}\lambda_0 p_0 x_0, \quad \phi_1 = \lambda_1 p_1 x_1$$

so

$$g_0, g_1 \geq 0, \quad \phi_0, \phi_1 > 0$$

and

$$g_0 x_1 = g_1 x_0,$$

and also

$$g_0 x_0 g_1 x_1 - g_0 x_1 g_1 x_0 = \lambda_0 \lambda_1 (p_0 x_0 p_1 x_1 - p_0 x_1 p_1 x_0) < 0.$$

Then with

$$G = \begin{pmatrix} g_0 \\ g_1 \end{pmatrix}, \quad X = (x_0, x_1), \quad H = G'(GX)^{-1}G,$$

the homogeneous quadratic

$$\Phi(x) = \tfrac{1}{2}x'Hx'$$

is as required for local compatibility, by Theorem 4.2, and then with
Theorem 4.3 the proof is complete.

APPENDIX[*]

*Based on a paper presented with John Kuiper at the Third World Congress of the Econometric Society, Toronto, 20-26 August 1975.

I. TOTAL AND INCREMENTAL INFLATION RATES AND INFLATION BIAS

In base and current periods $0, 1$ when prices are $p_0, p_1 \in \Omega_n$ a bundle of consumption goods $x \in \Omega^n$ has costs $M_0 = p_0 x$, $M_1 = p_1 x$. Then it is associated with a *Fleetwood point* $(M_0, M_1) \in \Omega \times \Omega$ and an *inflation rate* $R_{10} = M_1/M_0$. To assure that consumption can be maintained undisturbed by the price change, a household consuming x in the base-period, so the income is M_0, must have an inflation adjustment with this rate, giving $M_1 = R_{10} M_0$ as current income. Fleetwood showed this principle in 1707.

The original *inflation map* for a collection of households, from which further maps will be derived, is the set of all Fleetwood points, one for each household. It determines an average point $(\bar{M}_0, \bar{M}_1)$. Then $\bar{R}_{10} = \bar{M}_1/\bar{M}_0$ is the average inflation rate, associated with the average consumption bundle and it is identical with the *total inflation rate* associated with the total bundle for the collection.

The CPI is identical algebraically with the total inflation rate $\bar{R}_{10}$ determined from a sample of households. As such it is an estimate of that rate for the population, or the "target group". An everyday use of the CPI is to apply this rate uniformly to every income, as a social norm for inflation adjustments. In other words it is used *as if* it were a price index which, by the meaning of the concept, provides

a homogeneous linear relation $M_1 = \bar{P}_{10}M_0$ between incomes which at

the different prices have the same purchasing power, the index being

the slope. According to the criterion given by the original inflation

map, this procedure gives a correct total inflation adjustment, because

$\bar{M}_1 = \bar{R}_{10}\bar{M}_0$. But since every household has its own generally different

inflation rate, the distribution of this total is generally incorrect.

However, a criterion of correctness which distinguished every household

is not wanted. The principle already implicit in both theory and

practice is that the norm for the inflation adjustment of an income

should depend continuously on just the income. Let the population be

stratified into, say, 2^k income classes of equal size (k = 0 or 1

or ...). The number k describes the *degree* of stratification,

obtained by repeated bisections. When these strata are suitably narrow

or the degree is high, the inflation rates within any one are in principle

close to each other and represented statistically by the average

inflation rate in it. The stratification determines a partition of the

Fleetwood points in the original inflation map with 2^k classes, and

correspondingly determines 2^k average Fleetwood points, say (M_0^i, M_1^i)

(i = 1, ..., 2^k). Then $R_{10}^i = M_1^i/M_0^i$ is an estimate of the average

(and total) inflation rate for the ith stratum. It specifies a correct

total adjustment for each of the 2^k income strata.

Thus from the original inflation map with one point for each house-

hold is derived a map with one point for each of 2^k income strata.

One such map for some k (e.g. k = 1, 2, 3, or 4, giving 2, 4, 8, or

16 classes) is constructed as a *basic inflation map,* providing a basic

criterion for correct distribution of inflation adjustments. Then

from this map, by consolidating the strata in consecutive pairs into

2^{k-1} strata of twice the size, with the simple operation of

replacing the corresponding pairs of Fleetwood points by their mid-

point, the next coarser map of degree k-1 is obtained. By repeating

this process finally the maps with stratifications 1 and 0 are

derived. The last consists of a single point $(\bar{M}_0, \bar{M}_1)$, giving

$\bar{R}_{01} = \bar{M}_1/\bar{M}_0$ as an estimate of the average (and total) inflation rate

in the entire population, this being the same as the CPI.

Considering the usual homogeneous procedure in which the CPI is used

as a price index, for this to give the correct results as specified by

the basic k-map the condition is

$$R_{10}^i = \bar{R}_{01} \quad \text{for all} \quad i.$$

But this is just the condition for all the points (M_0^i, M_1^i) in the

basic k-map to lie on the same ray. Usually on the contrary there will

be different inflation rates R_{10}^i in all the strata $i = 1, \ldots, 2^k$,

lying generally anywhere between the maximum and minimum of the price-

ratios p_{1r}/p_{0r} (r = 1, ..., n) for the individual goods.

The series of maps k, k-1, ..., 0 provide a series of decreasingly

fine distribution criteria for the inflation adjustment of income. The

last, the 0-criterion, specifies just the total. Next to that the

1-criterion specifies also how this total should be divided between the

upper and lower halves, where incomes are above and below the median.

The procedure with the CPI corresponds to adopting $M_1 = \bar{R}_{10}M_0$ as the

relation between equivalent incomes. The graph is a ray in the Fleetwood

space through the average point $(\bar{M}_0, \bar{M}_1)$. It can be called the average price index or API-ray (it being understood that API = CPI = average inflation rate = total inflation rate). From this, and as already seen, it meets the 0-criterion. In fact any line through the average point $(\bar{M}_0, \bar{M}_1)$, that is any relation

$$M_1 - \bar{M}_1 = S_{10}(M_0 - \bar{M}_0)$$

will meet the 0-criterion about the total inflation adjustment. But there is *just one,* for a particular value of S_{10}, which moreover meets the 1-criterion about how the total is divided between upper and lower halves of the population. This is obtained by joining the two Fleetwood points in the 1-map, which are the average points for incomes above and below the median. It can be called the marginal price index or MPI-line. Its slope S_{10} defines the *incremental inflation rate* (= marginal price index).

The sense of this is that if incomes are to be adjusted from the base period to the current period by a linear relation meeting criteria about the total inflation adjustment and about the division of this total between the upper and lower halves of the population, this is done by adjusting the total by the total inflation rate R_{10}, and adjusting the spacing of the incomes by the incremental inflation rate S_{10}.

From another point of view, these two rates are two independent paramaters for examining income distribution, taxation, and related norms or policies, and so also, when refinements are needed, are these rates which are associated with each class in any stratification. Of cardinal interest is the computed difference between the overall total and incremental inflation rates. The sign of this gives a distinction between *high bias* and *low bias inflation.* The ratio $B_{10} = S_{10}/R_{10}$ can

define the *inflation bias index*. In the high bias case the usual
homogeneous procedure with CPI will have a bias in favour of low
incomes and against high incomes, and vice versa in the opposite case.
For many indexation purposes it is the incremental rate alone which is
relevant. In a similar way inflation maps can be constructed with
reference to other distinctions beside income class, such as regional,
occupational, family characteristics, cities, and so forth.

I am indebted to Professor Irene Spry, of the University of Ottawa,
whose objection to the ambiguous "marginal" instead of "incremental"
influenced a change in terminology. The average and marginal price
indices, API and MPI, have become the total and incremental inflation
rates. An immediacy in the sense of the terms entering social and
political interests comes from a remark of Mr. E.J. van Goudoever, of
Health and Welfare Canada, about the incremental rate: while the total
rate affects the total level of incomes, the incremental rate affects
the spacing between them, or the increments between the ranks. This
change in terminology, and the reference to a basic inflation map as
the origin for all construction, assists a release from the habit of
thinking in terms of homogeneous price indices. Nevertheless the API
and MPI terminology fits in with a usage which is familiar in theory of
the firm and has a counterpart in the theory of index numbers. The
scheme described embodies its own theory and requires no further
conceptual explanation. But it can still be explained and elaborated
further by being placed in a framework where price index and marginal
price index appear as particular concepts and the API and MPI are
constructed specifically as such.

FIGURE 15

Inflation Maps : Income Groups

Successive enlargements of information:

   (i)   the API (= CPI)

  (ii) community average Fleetwood point F

 (iii) first disaggregation, giving also the MPI

  (iv) second disaggregation

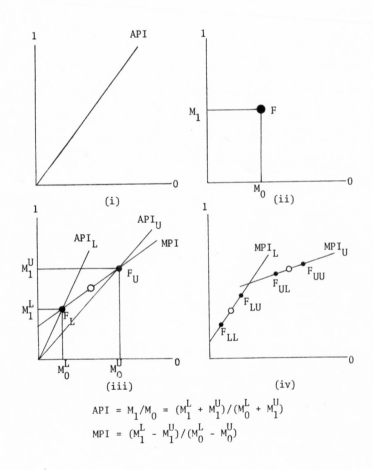

$$API = M_1/M_0 = (M_1^L + M_1^U)/(M_0^L + M_1^U)$$

$$MPI = (M_1^L - M_1^U)/(M_0^L - M_0^U)$$

II.   COMPUTATIONS : STATISTICS CANADA DATA

DATA:

(a)   Detailed average expenditures by 36 family income
groups, covering entire income range, all Canada, ur-
banization classes, families and unattached individuals.
656 items including subtotals, 1969.

(b)   Consumer price indices for Canada, complete monthly
series.   455 items, 1969 base.

COMPUTER:

IBM 360-65 at the University of Ottawa Computing Centre,
using the MATOP package developed by John Kuiper (1974).

TABLES

INFLATION RATES, INCREMENTAL RATES

AND INFLATION BIAS

Tables for the entire expenditure range

for the following income stratifications:

I   *by approximate octiles*

II   "   "   *quartiles*

III   "   "   *median bisection*

IV   *overall*

comprising in each case tables for:

(a) *total current consumption at the prices in each year 1961-1974 for each income group with 1969 standards*

(b) *inflation rates across each year for each income group*

(c) *corresponding incremental rates*

(d) *inflation bias*

NOTE

The *bias index,* in any income stratum, is given by

$$B = MPI/API .$$

The entries in the Tables (b) *and* (c) are

$$x = (API - 1)100 ,$$

$$y = (MPI - 1)100 ,$$

so

$$B = ((y/100) + 1)/((x/100) + 1)$$

$$= ((y/100) + 1)(1 - (x/100))$$

$$= ((y - x)/100) + 1$$

approximately, when x, y are small compared with 100. Thus, approximately,

$$(B - 1)100 = y - x,$$

and hence

$$z = (B - 1)100,$$

which is entered in Table (d), gives the approximation

$$z = y - x.$$

TABLE I

INCOME STRATIFICATION BY APPROXIMATE OCTILES

(a) TOTAL CURRENT CONSUMPTION (1969 STANDARDS)

	GROUP 1	GROUP 2	GROUP 3	GROUP 4	GROUP 5	GROUP 6	GROUP 7	GROUP 8
1961	1795.43	2987.53	4059.16	4939.93	5686.79	6346.50	7313.85	9632.65
1962	1814.33	3017.99	4098.69	4986.89	5742.55	6409.93	7385.88	9731.86
1963	1841.08	3062.04	4157.46	5056.81	5825.37	6503.60	7494.59	9880.98
1964	1866.97	3107.99	4221.22	5134.25	5917.08	6609.34	7617.20	10047.16
1965	1904.25	3173.31	4312.69	5246.57	6047.87	6755.51	7783.87	10261.93
1966	1975.34	3292.10	4471.39	5436.00	6267.02	6999.31	8062.14	10622.20
1967	2036.10	3398.02	4617.84	5613.97	6474.76	7237.27	8341.71	11009.42
1968	2110.24	3520.19	4783.52	5814.49	6707.67	7500.46	8643.51	11416.05
1969	2197.58	3662.86	4975.28	6046.51	6977.67	7806.42	8993.83	11889.35
1970	2266.71	3775.00	5128.06	6234.00	7198.65	8056.87	9284.18	12287.14
1971	2325.79	3871.50	5262.15	6401.04	7397.80	8289.98	9552.64	12668.65
1972	2437.38	4050.62	5497.96	6685.95	7730.21	8663.55	9975.16	13230.22
1973	2627.88	4355.28	5891.58	7155.80	8275.86	9270.04	10657.20	14110.24
1974	2916.96	4832.20	6535.60	7932.41	9177.99	10278.21	11812.70	15631.40

(b) INFLATION RATES

	GROUP 1	GROUP 2	GROUP 3	GROUP 4	GROUP 5	GROUP 6	GROUP 7	GROUP 8
1961-62	1.1	1.0	1.0	1.0	1.0	1.0	1.0	1.0
1962-63	1.5	1.5	1.4	1.4	1.4	1.5	1.5	1.5
1963-64	1.4	1.5	1.5	1.5	1.6	1.6	1.6	1.7
1964-65	2.0	2.1	2.2	2.2	2.2	2.2	2.2	2.1
1965-66	3.7	3.7	3.7	3.6	3.6	3.6	3.6	3.5
1966-67	3.1	3.2	3.3	3.3	3.3	3.4	3.5	3.6
1967-68	3.6	3.6	3.6	3.6	3.6	3.6	3.6	3.7
1968-69	4.1	4.1	4.0	4.0	4.0	4.1	4.1	4.1
1969-70	3.1	3.1	3.1	3.1	3.2	3.2	3.2	3.3
1970-71	2.6	2.6	2.6	2.7	2.8	2.9	2.9	3.1
1971-72	4.8	4.6	4.5	4.5	4.5	4.5	4.4	4.4
1972-73	7.8	7.5	7.2	7.0	7.1	7.0	6.8	6.7
1973-74	11.0	11.0	10.9	10.9	10.9	10.9	10.8	10.8

(c) INCREMENTAL RATES

	GROUP 1	GROUP 2	GROUP 3	GROUP 4	GROUP 5	GROUP 6	GROUP 7	GROUP 8
1961-62	0.8	0.8	0.9	0.5	0.7	0.7	0.6	1.0
1962-63	1.2	1.4	1.2	1.2	1.3	1.3	1.2	1.6
1963-64	1.1	1.6	2.6	0.9	1.3	1.0	2.2	1.4
1964-65	2.1	2.3	2.6	1.4	1.9	1.5	2.1	1.8
1965-66	3.3	3.5	3.8	2.5	2.9	2.4	3.1	3.1
1966-67	3.1	3.7	3.4	3.5	3.7	3.7	4.1	4.0
1967-68	3.3	3.6	3.5	3.3	3.5	3.4	3.0	3.8
1968-69	3.9	3.7	3.7	3.8	3.7	3.5	3.5	4.2
1969-70	3.0	2.8	3.0	3.2	3.3	3.0	2.7	3.6
1970-71	2.9	2.4	1.9	2.9	3.2	3.2	2.3	3.8
1971-72	4.6	3.6	3.9	3.6	3.7	4.2	2.8	4.4
1972-73	7.3	5.9	7.2	4.9	5.3	5.8	4.6	5.8
1973-74	11.1	10.5	10.6	9.3	10.6	10.3	9.3	10.5

(d) INFLATION BIAS

	GROUP 1	GROUP 2	GROUP 3	GROUP 4	GROUP 5	GROUP 6	GROUP 7	GROUP 8
1961-62	-0.2	-0.3	-0.1	-0.4	-0.3	-0.3	-0.3	0.0
1962-63	-0.3	-0.0	-0.2	-0.2	-0.1	-0.2	-0.2	0.1
1963-64	-0.3	0.1	1.1	-0.6	-0.3	-0.5	0.6	-0.1
1964-65	0.1	0.2	0.5	-0.7	-0.3	-0.6	-0.1	-0.4
1965-66	-0.4	-0.3	0.1	-1.1	-0.7	-1.3	-0.5	-0.6
1966-67	0.0	0.4	0.1	0.2	0.4	0.5	0.8	0.7
1967-68	-0.4	0.0	-0.1	-0.3	-0.1	-0.2	-0.6	0.2
1968-69	-0.3	-0.3	-0.3	-0.2	-0.4	-0.6	-0.5	0.2
1969-70	-0.1	-0.2	-0.1	0.1	0.1	-0.1	-0.4	0.4
1970-71	0.2	-0.2	-0.7	0.2	0.4	0.6	-0.4	1.1
1971-72	-0.2	-0.9	-0.5	-0.8	-0.7	-0.4	-1.5	-0.2
1972-73	-0.5	-1.4	0.0	-2.0	-1.7	-1.6	-2.3	-1.4
1973-74	0.1	-0.4	-0.3	-1.4	-0.2	-0.6	-1.4	-0.4

TABLE II

INCOME STRATIFICATION BY APPROXIMATE QUARTILES

(a) TOTAL CURRENT CONSUMPTION (1969 STANDARDS)

	GROUP 1	GROUP 2	GROUP 3	GROUP 4
1961	2442.37	4537.82	5986.02	8446.85
1962	2467.54	4581.38	6045.26	8532.15
1963	2503.68	4646.21	6133.00	8660.61
1964	2540.46	4717.41	6231.08	8804.51
1965	2592.95	4820.20	6368.84	8994.68
1966	2689.92	4995.61	6599.18	9313.02
1967	2775.19	5159.19	6820.63	9645.18
1968	2875.40	5343.80	7067.27	9998.21
1969	2992.76	5557.43	7353.58	10408.62
1970	3085.23	5729.08	7588.83	10751.46
1971	3164.63	5881.08	7802.48	11075.16
1972	3312.86	6143.57	8153.56	11565.62
1973	3564.23	6578.62	8726.81	12344.40
1974	3956.33	7294.69	9677.03	13678.56

(b) INFLATION RATES

	GROUP 1	GROUP 2	GROUP 3	GROUP 4
1961-62	1.0	1.0	1.0	1.0
1962-63	1.5	1.4	1.5	1.5
1963-64	1.5	1.5	1.6	1.7
1964-65	2.1	2.2	2.2	2.2
1965-66	3.7	3.6	3.6	3.5
1966-67	3.2	3.3	3.4	3.6
1967-68	3.6	3.6	3.6	3.7
1968-69	4.1	4.0	4.1	4.1
1969-70	3.1	3.1	3.2	3.3
1970-71	2.6	2.7	2.8	3.0
1971-72	4.7	4.5	4.5	4.4
1972-73	7.6	7.1	7.0	6.7
1973-74	11.0	10.9	10.9	10.8

(c) INCREMENTAL RATES

	GROUP 1	GROUP 2	GROUP 3	GROUP 4
1961-62	1.0	0.8	1.2	1.2
1962-63	1.4	1.3	1.6	1.7
1963-64	1.6	1.5	2.1	1.8
1964-65	2.3	2.3	2.2	2.0
1965-66	3.8	3.3	3.5	3.3
1966-67	3.4	3.3	4.1	4.2
1967-68	3.5	3.5	4.0	3.9
1968-69	3.9	3.9	4.5	4.4
1969-70	2.9	3.2	3.8	3.7
1970-71	2.5	3.0	3.7	3.8
1971-72	4.4	4.3	4.6	4.5
1972-73	7.0	6.4	6.5	6.1
1973-74	11.0	10.5	10.7	10.6

(d) INFLATION BIAS

	GROUP 1	GROUP 2	GROUP 3	GROUP 4
1961-62	-0.1	-0.1	0.2	0.2
1962-63	-0.0	-0.2	0.2	0.2
1963-64	0.2	-0.0	0.5	0.2
1964-65	0.2	0.1	0.0	-0.2
1965-66	0.0	-0.3	-0.1	-0.2
1966-67	0.3	-0.0	0.7	0.6
1967-68	-0.1	-0.1	0.3	0.3
1968-69	-0.2	-0.1	0.5	0.3
1969-70	-0.1	0.1	0.6	0.4
1970-71	-0.1	0.3	0.9	0.7
1971-72	-0.3	-0.1	0.1	0.0
1972-73	-0.6	-0.6	-0.5	-0.6
1973-74	0.0	-0.4	-0.2	-0.2

TABLE III

(a) APPROXIMATE MEDIAN INCOME STRATIFICATION

TOTAL CURRENT CONSUMPTION (1969 STANDARDS)

	GROUP 1	GROUP 2
1961	3442.28	7272.99
1962	3476.23	7345.87
1963	3526.06	7454.90
1964	3579.26	7576.94
1965	3655.76	7742.11
1966	3790.16	8018.47
1967	3912.80	8297.82
1968	4053.28	8600.10
1969	4216.59	8951.31
1970	4346.84	9242.84
1971	4460.88	9514.04
1972	4663.63	9938.01
1973	5002.65	10618.75
1974	5549.35	11769.77

(b) INFLATION RATES

	GROUP 1	GROUP 2
1961-62	1.0	1.0
1962-63	1.4	1.5
1963-64	1.5	1.6
1964-65	2.1	2.2
1965-66	3.7	3.6
1966-67	3.2	3.5
1967-68	3.6	3.6
1968-69	4.0	4.1
1969-70	3.1	3.3
1970-71	2.6	2.9
1971-72	4.5	4.5
1972-73	7.3	6.8
1973-74	10.9	10.8

(c) INCREMENTAL RATES

	GROUP 1	GROUP 2
1961-62	0.9	1.1
1962-63	1.4	1.6
1963-64	1.6	1.8
1964-65	2.3	2.0
1965-66	3.5	3.4
1966-67	3.4	4.1
1967-68	3.5	3.8
1968-69	3.9	4.2
1969-70	3.1	3.5
1970-71	2.7	3.5
1971-72	4.2	4.3
1972-73	6.5	6.0
1973-74	10.7	10.6

(d) INFLATION BIAS

	GROUP 1	GROUP 2
1961-62	-0.1	0.1
1962-63	-0.1	0.2
1963-64	0.1	0.2
1964-65	0.2	-0.1
1965-66	-0.1	-0.2
1966-67	0.2	0.6
1967-68	-0.0	0.1
1968-69	-0.1	0.1
1969-70	-0.0	0.3
1970-71	0.1	0.5
1971-72	-0.3	-0.2
1972-73	-0.7	-0.8
1973-74	-0.2	-0.2

TABLE IV

ALL INCOME GROUPS

(a) TOTAL CURRENT CONSUMPTION (1969 STANDARDS)

	TOTAL
1961	5277.91
1962	5330.51
1963	5408.71
1964	5494.90
1965	5613.89
1966	5816.31
1967	6014.05
1968	6232.06
1969	6485.41
1970	6692.94
1971	6882.29
1972	7191.05
1973	7693.81
1974	8530.09

(b) INFLATION RATES

	TOTAL
1961-62	1.0
1962-63	1.5
1963-64	1.6
1964-65	2.2
1965-66	3.6
1566-67	3.4
1967-68	3.6
1968-69	4.1
1969-70	3.2
1970-71	2.8
1971-72	4.5
1972-73	7.0
1973-74	10.9

(c) INCREMENTAL RATES

	TOTAL
1961-62	1.0
1962-63	1.5
1963-64	1.8
1964-65	2.2
1965-66	3.5
1966-67	3.7
1967-68	3.7
1968-69	4.1
1969-70	3.4
1970-71	3.2
1971-72	4.4
1972-73	6.5
1973-74	10.8

(d) INFLATION BIAS

	TOTAL
1961-62	0.0
1962-63	0.1
1963-64	0.2
1964-65	0.1
1965-66	-0.1
1966-67	0.3
1967-68	0.1
1968-69	0.1
1969-70	0.2
1970-71	0.4
1971-72	-0.1
1972-73	-0.5
1973-74	-0.1

NOTATION

Ω the non-negative numbers

Ω^n the space of non-negative column vectors with n elements, *the commodity space*

Ω_n the same except with row vectors, the price space, or *the budget space*

any $x \in \Omega^n$, $p \in \Omega_n$ determine $px \in \Omega$, *the value of the bundle of goods* x *at the prices* p

$[x : H(x)]$ the set of x for which the statement $H(x)$ is true

$\wedge$, $\vee$ *conjunction, disjunction* ("and", "or")

$\underset{x}{\wedge} H(x)$ alternatively $(\wedge x)H(x)$, asserts $H(x)$ for all x, or that *the set* $[x : H(x)]$ *includes every considered element*

$\underset{x}{\vee} H(x)$ or $(\vee x)H(x)$, asserts $H(x)$ for some x, or that *the set* $[x : H(x)]$ *is not empty*

punctuation   in $A \wedge B .=>. C$ shows that $(A \wedge B) => C$ is meant, and not $A \wedge (B => C)$ which would be $A. \wedge .B => C$ *a comma is often used in place of* $\wedge$, thus $A, B .=>. C$

$H(x) => K(x)$ *since* x *appears on both sides* is understood to mean $(\wedge x) . H(x) => K(x)$, the same as $(\wedge H(x))K(x)$, and as $\underset{H(x)}{\wedge} K(x)$, and *asserts* $K(x)$ *for all* x *such that* $H(x)$

$R \subset S \times S$ a *binary relation* in a set S

xRy x *has the relation* R *to* y, means $(x, y) \in R$

$\overline{R}$ the *complement*, $x\overline{R}y$ denies xRy

R' the *converse*, $xR'y$ asserts yRx

$\overrightarrow{R}$ the *transitive closure*, $x\overrightarrow{R}y$ asserts $xRz_1Rz_2\ldots Ry$ for some $z_1, z_2, \ldots$

Rx the set $[y : yRx]$ of elements *which have the relation* R *to* x

xR the set $[y : xRy]$ of elements *to which* x *has the relation* R

BIBLIOGRAPHY

I. List of earlier sources and related materials of author

On Linear Differential Forms and the Symmetry Condition of Slutsky.
The Consistency Condition and Other Concepts in the Theory of Value and
Demand.
The Calculation of Index Numbers of the Standard and Cost of Living.
On Index Numbers in the Theory of Value and Demand.
Theory of Economic Index Numbers.
Department of Applied Economics, Cambridge, 1956. (unpublished)

Preferences and the Theory of Consumers' Expenditures.
Washington Meeting of the Econometric Society, December 1959.
Abstract in *Econometrica* 28, 3 (1960), 693-695.

The Analysis of Preferences.
Research Memorandum No. 11 (January 1960). Econometric Research
Program, Princeton University.

Preference Scales and Expenditure Systems.
Research Memorandum No. 13 (March 1960). Econometric Research
Program, Princeton University. *Econometrica* 30 (1962), 305-323.

The System of Inequalities $a_{rs} > X_r - X_s$.
Research Memorandum No. 18 (October 1960). Econometric Research
Program, Princeton University. *Proc. Cambridge Phil. Soc.* 59 (1963),
125-133.

Gradient Configurations and Quadratic Functions.
Research Memorandum No. 20 (January 1961). Econometric Research
Program, Princeton University. *Proc. Cambridge Phil. Soc.* 59 (1963),
287-305.

Expenditure Configurations.
Research Memorandum No. 21 (February 1961). Econometric Research
Program, Princeton University.

The Cost of Living Index.
Research Memoranda Nos. 24 (March 1961), 27 (April 1961), and 29
(August 1961). Econometric Research Program, Princeton University.
Presented at the Stillwater Meeting of the Econometric Society,
August 1961. Partial abstract in *Econometrica* 30, 2 (1962): 357.
No. 29 published in *Studies in Mathematical Economics in Honor of
Oskar Morgenstern,* ed. by Martin Shubik, Chapter 23, 335-365.
Princeton University Press, 1967.

The Conceptual Problem of a Cost of Living Index.
Stanford Meeting of the Econometric Society, August 1960. Abstract
in *Econometrica* 29, 3 (1961), 440.

A Formula for Ranging the Cost of Living.
   Abstract in R.L. Graves and P. Wolfe (eds.) *Recent Advances in*
   Mathematical Programming, Proceedings of the Chicago Symposium.
   New York: McGraw-Hill, 1962.

The Algebra of Revealed Preference.
   Pittsburgh Meeting of the Econometric Society, December 1962.
   Abstract in *Econometrica* 31, 4 (1963), 755.

An Identity Concerning the Relation between the Paasche and Laspeyres
   Indices.
   Metroeconomica 15, 2-3 (1963), 136-140.

On Bernoullian Utility for Goods and Money.
   Metroeconomica 15, 1 (1963), 38-46.

The Method of Limits in the Theory of Index Numbers.
   Joint European Conference of the Institute of Mathematical Statistics
   and the Econometric Society, Copenhagen, July 1963. *Metroeconomica*
   21, 2 (1969), 141-165.

The Construction of Utility Functions from Expenditure Data.
   Cowles Foundation Discussion Paper No. 144 (October 1964), Yale
   University. Presented at the First World Congress of the Econometric
   Society, Rome, September 1965. *International Economic Review* 8, 1
   (1967), 67-77.

Principles of Choice and Preference.
   Research Paper No. 160 (February 1967), Department of Economics,
   Purdue University.

The Construction of Cost-efficiencies and Approximate Utility Functions
   from Inconsistent Expenditure Data.
   New York Meeting of the Econometric Society, December 1969.

The Concept of a Price Index and its Extension.
   Second World Congress of the Econometric Society, Cambridge, August
   1970.

The Cost and Utility of Consumption.
Direct and Indirect Utility.
National Capacity Comparison.
   Department of Economics, University of North Carolina at Chapel Hill,
   1970. (unpublished)

Theory of Maxima and the Method of Lagrange.
   Journal of Applied Mathematics 20, 3 (May 1971), 343-357.

A Macroanalysis of Shubik's Curmudgeon Guide.
   December 1971, unpublished.

The Case of the Vanishing Slutsky Matrix.
Journal of Economic Theory 5, 2 (October 1972), 208-223.

The Theory of Comparisons of Real Income and Prices.
In D.J. Daly (ed.), *International Comparisons of Prices and Output*,
Proceedings of the National Bureau of Economic Research Conference
at York University, Toronto, 1970. NBER Studies in Income and Wealth
Vol. 37, 13-84. Columbia University Press, 1972.

On a System of Inequalities in Demand Analysis: an Extension of the
Classical Method.
International Economic Review 14, 2 (June 1973), 460-472.

Adam Smith and Robinson Crusoe: A note following the celebrations of
the 250th birthday of Adam Smith at Kircaldy, Scotland, 4-5 June,
1973, dedicated to Sir Roy Harrod, Chairman of the Symposium.

A General Defect with Price Indices and a Simple Remedy.
Atlantic Economic Conference, Richmond, Virginia, September 28-29,
1973.

Sum-symmetric Matrices.
Linear Algebra and its Applications 8 (1974), 129-140.

Measurement of the Purchasing Power of Incomes with Linear Expansion
Data. *Journal of Econometrics* 2, 3 (1974), 343-364.

Review of *The Effect of Education on Efficiency in Consumption* by
Robert T. Michael.
Monthly Labour Review 97, 1 (January 1974), 86-87.

Collective Decision and Optimality.
International Seminar in Public Economics, Siena, Italy, 3-6
September, 1973. *Proceedings* edited by R. Musgrave, ISPE c/o Department
of Economics, Harvard University, 1974.

The Variable Impact of Inflation on Purchasing Power at Different Levels
of Income.
National Bureau of Economic Research Conference on the Analysis of
Consumer Expenditure Data, NBER West Coast Center, Palo Alto,
California, 2-3 May, 1974.

Reservations about Market Sovereignty: Four Notes.
In *Policy Formation in an Open Economy: The Case of Canada*.
Proceedings of the Conference held at the University of Waterloo,
11-14 November, 1972. Vol. 2, 485-493. Waterloo, Ontario: The
Waterloo Research Institute, 1974.

The Collective Optimum.
Discussion Paper 7409 (October), Department of Economics, University
of Ottawa.

The Marginal Price Index Method.
Discussion Paper No. 7415, Department of Economics, University of
Ottawa.

Sraffa's Prices.
Discussion Paper 7511 (April), Department of Economics, University of
Ottawa.

(with John Kuiper)
Inflation Maps and the Total and Incremental Inflation Rates.
Third World Congress of the Econometric Society, Toronto, 20-26
August, 1975.

Democratic Order Functions.
Atlantic Economic Journal 3, 2 (November 1975), 13-21.

Demand Functions and the Slutsky Matrix.
1976, unpublished.

On Wald's "New Formula" for the Cost of Living.
International Seminar on the Theory and Applications of Economic
Indices, Karlsruhe, 23 June-1 July, 1976. *Proceedings* edited by
W. Eichhorn, Physica-Verlag, forthcoming.

Combinatorial Theory of Demand.
London: Input-Output Publishing Co., 1976.

II. General Bibliography

Allen, R.G.D.: The Economic Theory of Index Numbers. *Economica*, New Series 16, 63 (August 1949), 197-203.

——— Index Numbers of Volume and Price, in *International Trade Statistics*, ed. R.G.D. Allen and J. Edward Ely. New York, 1953.

——— Price Index Numbers. *International Statistical Review* 31 (1963), 281-301.

——— *Index Numbers in Theory and Practice*. London: Macmillan, 1975.

Allen, R.G.D., and A.L. Bowley: *Family Expenditure*. London, 1935.

Antonelli, G.B.: *Sulla Teoria Matematica della Economia Pura* (1886). Reprinted in *Giornale degli Economisti* 10 (1951), 233-263.

Arrow, K.J.: The Measurement of Real Value Added. Technical Report 60, IMSSS, Stanford University, California, 1972.

Banerjee, Kali S.: *Cost of Living Index Numbers*. New York: Marcel Dekker, 1975.

Bergson, A.: *National Income of the Soviet Union Since 1928*. Cambridge, Massachusetts: Harvard University Press, 1961.

Bowley, A.L.: Review of *The Making of Index Numbers* by Irving Fisher. *Economic Journal* 33 (1923), 90-94.

——— Notes on Index Numbers. *Economic Journal* 38 (June 1928), 216-237.

Brown, J.A.C., and A. Deaton: Models of Consumer Behaviour: A Survey. *Economic Journal* 82 (1972), 1145-1236.

Buscheguennce, S.S.: Sur une classe des hypersurfaces: à propos de 'l'index idéal' de M. Irving Fischer. *Recueil Mathématique* (Moscow) 32 (1925), 625-631. (Russian title: Byushgens, S.S., Ob odnom klasse giperpoverkhnostey: po povodu 'idealnovo indeksa' Irving Fischer' a pokupatelnoi sili deneg. *Mathematischeskii Sbornik* 32 (1925), 625-631.)

Carli, G.R.: Del Valore etc. *Opere Scelte,* 1764, Vol. 1, p. 299.

Carter, C.F., W.B. Reddaway, and Richard Stone: *The Measurement of Production Movements*. Cambridge University Press, 1948.

Central Statistical Office: *Method of Construction and Calculation of the Index of Retail Prices,* Studies in Official Statistics, No. 6,

4th ed. H.M. Statistical Office, 1967.

——— *National Accounts Statistics, Sources and Methods,* 2nd ed. H.M. Statistical Office, 1970.

Chase, Arnold E.: Concepts and Uses of Price Indices. Paper presented at the American Statistical Association meeting, August 1960.

Christensen, L.R. and D.W. Jorgensen: U.S. Real Product and Real Factor Output, 1929-1967. *Review of Income and Wealth* 16 (1970), 19-50.

Cournot, A.: *Recherches sur les Principes Mathématiques de la Théorie des Richesses.* Paris: L. Hachette, 1838. (*Researches into the Mathematical Principles of the Theory of Wealth.* Trans. by N.T. Bacon, with an Essay on Cournot and a Bibliography on mathematical economics by I. Fisher, 1924. New York: Kelley Reprints of Economic Classics, 1960.)

Craig, J.: On the Elementary Treatment of Index Numbers, *Journal of the Royal Statistical Society* C 18 (1969), 141-152.

Crowe, W.R.: *Index Numbers - Theory and Applications.* London 1965.

Davidson, A.: *Money in the Real World.* London: Macmillan, 1974.

Diewert, W.E.: Afriat and Revealed Preference Theory. *Review of Economic Studies* 40 (1973), 419-425.

——— Exact and Superlative Index Numbers. *Journal of Econometrics* 4 (1976), 115-145.

Divisia, F.: L'Indice Monétaire et la Théorie de la Monnaie. *Revue d'Economie Politique* 39 (1925), 980-1008.

——— L'Indice Monétaire et la Théorie de la Monnaie. Societe anonyme du Recueil Sirley, Paris, 1926.

——— *Economique Rationelle.* Paris, 1928.

Dobb, Maurice: *Welfare Economics and the Economics of Socialism.* Cambridge University Press, 1969.

Edgeworth, F.Y.: A Defence of Index Numbers. *Economic Journal* (1896), 132-142.

——— Third report of the British Association Committee for the purpose of investigating the best methods of ascertaining and measuring variation in the value of the monetary standard. 1889.

——— *Papers Relating to Political Economy,* Vol. 1. London, 1925.

———— The Plurality of Index Numbers. *Economic Journal* 35 (1925), 379-388.

Eichhorn, Wolfgang: Zur axiomatischen Theorie des Preisindex. *Demonstratio Mathematica* 6 (1973), 561-573.

———— Fischer's Tests Revisited. *Econometrica* 44, 2 (March 1976), 247-256.

Engel, E.: Die Productions und Consumptionsverhaltnisse des Konigreichs Sachsen, reprinted in *Bulletin de l'Institut International de Statistique* 9 Appendix (1857, 1895).

Fisher, Irving: *The Purchasing Power of Money*. New York: Macmillan, 1911.

———— *The Making of Index Numbers*. Boston: Houghton Mifflin, 1922.

———— Professor Bowley on Index Numbers. *Economic Journal* 33 (1923), 246-251.

———— A Statistical Method for Measuring Marginal Utility and Testing the Justice of a Progressive Income Tax. In *Economic Essays in Honor of John Bates Clark*. New York, 1927.

Fisher, F.M. and K. Shell: Taste and Quality Change in the Pure Theory of the True Cost of Living Index. In *Value, Capital and Growth, Papers in Honor of Sir John Hicks*, ed. by J.N. Wolfe. Edinburgh University Press, 1968.

———— *The Economic Theory of Price Indices*. New York: Academic Press, 1972.

Fisher, W.C.: The Tabular Standard in Massachusetts. *Quarterly Journal of Economics*, May 1913.

Fleetwood, William: *Chronicon Preciosum: or, an Account of English Money, The Price of Corn, and Other Commodities, for the last 600 Years - in a Letter to a Student in the University of Oxford*. London, 1707.

Foster, William T.: Prefatory Note to *The Making of Index Numbers* by Irving Fisher (see above).

Fowler, R.F.: *Some Problems of Index Number Construction*. Studies in Official Statistics, Research Series, No. 3. H.M. Statistical Office, 1970.

Fowler, R.F.: Further Problems of Index Number Construction. Studies in Official Statistics, Research Series, No. 5. H.M. Statistical Office, 1973.

———— An Ambiguity in the Terminology of Index Number Construction. *Journal of the Royal Statistical Society* A 137 (1974), 75-88.

Frisch, Ragnar: Necessary and Sufficient Conditions Regarding the Form on an Index Number Which Shall Meet Certain of Fisher's Tests. *Journal of the American Statistical Association* 25 (1930), 397-406.

———— Annual Survey of General Economic Theory: The Problem of Index Numbers. *Econometrica* 4, 1 (1936), 1-39.

———— Some Basic Principles of Price of Living Measurements: A Survey Article. *Econometrica* 22 (1954), 407-421.

Galbraith, J.K.: *Money*. Cambridge, Mass.: Houghton Mifflin, 1975.

Gamaletsos, T.: Further Analysis of Cross-Country Comparison of Consumer Expenditure Patterns. *European Economic Review* 4 (1973), 1-20.

Geary, R.C.: A Note on a Constant-utility Index of the Cost of Living. *Review of Economic Studies* 18 (1950), 64-66.

Georgescu-Roegen, N.: Choice and Revealed Preference. *Southern Economic Journal* 21 (1954), 119-130.

———— Analytical Economics: Issues and Problems. Cambridge, Massachusetts: Harvard University Press, 1966.

Gorman, W.M.: Community Preference Fields. *Econometrica* 21 (1953), 63-80.

———— On a Class of Preference Fields. *Metroeconomica* 13 (1961), 53-56.

Gossling, W.F.: *Some Productive Consequences of Engel's Law*. London: Input-Output Publishing Co., 1974. (Occasional Paper No. 2).

Green, H.A.J.: *Aggregation in Economic Analysis*. Princeton University Press, 1964.

Griliches, Z.: (ed.) *Price Indexes and Quality Change - Studies in New Methods of Measurement*. Cambridge, Massachusetts: Harvard University Press, 1971.

Haberler, B. von: *Der Sinn der Indexzahlen*. Tubingen, 1927.

Hasenkamp, Georg: A Note on the Cost-of-Living Index. University of Bonn, January 1976. Presented at the European Meeting of the Econometric Society, Helsinki, August 1976.

Hicks, J.R.: Consumers' surplus and index-numbers. *Review of Economic Studies* 9, 2 (1942), 126-137.

————   *Value and Capital,* 2nd ed.   Oxford: The Clarendon Press,
1948.

————   *A Revision of Demand Theory.*   Oxford: The Clarendon Press,
1956.

Hicks, J.R., and R.G.D. Allen: A reconsideration of the theory of
value. *Economica,* New Series 1 (1934), 52-75, 196-219.

Hofsten, E. von: Witchcraft and Index Numbers. *Malayan Economic Review*
1 (1956), 6-14.

Hotelling, H.:   Demand functions with limited budgets. *Econometrica* 3
(1935), 66-78.

Houthakker, H.S.:   Revealed Preference and the Utility Function.
Economica, New Series 17 (1950), 159-174.

————   La forme des courbes d'Engel. *Cahiers du Seminarie d'Econometrie*
2 (1953), 59-66.

————   An International Comparison of Household Expenditure Patterns,
Commemorating the Centenary of Engel's Law. *Econometrica* 25 (1957),
532-551.

Ichimura, S.:   A Critical Note on the Definition of Related Goods.
Review of Economic Studies 18 (1951), 179-183.

Jazairi, N.T.:   An Empirical Study of the Conventional and Statistical
Theories of Index Numbers. *Oxford Institute of Economics and Statistics
Bulletin* 33 (1971), 181-195.

Jevons, W.S.:   *A serious fall in the value of gold ascertained and its
social effects set forth.*   London, 1863.

Kendall, M.G.:   The Early History of Index Numbers. *International
Statistical Review* 37 (1969), 1-12.

Keynes, J.M.:   *A Treatise on Money,* Vol. 1, *The Pure Theory of Money.*
New York: Harcourt, Brace, 1930.

————   *The General Theory of Employment, Interest, and Money.*
London: Macmillan, 1936.

Klein, L.R., and H. Rubin: A Constant Utility Index of the Cost of
Living. *Review of Economic Studies* 15 (1947), 84-87.

Kloek, T.:   *Indexcijfers: Enige methodologische aspecten.*   The Hague:
Pasmans, 1966.

————   On quadratic approximations of cost of living and real income

index numbers. *Report* 6710, Econometric Institute, Netherlands
School of Economics, Rotterdam, 1967.

Konyus, A.A.: Problema istinovo indeksa stoimosti zhizni. *Ekonomicheskii
Byulleten Konyunkturnovo Instituta* 3 (1924), 64-71. English trans.:
The Problem of the True Index of the Cost of Living. *Econometrica* 7
(Jan. 1939), 10-29.

Konyus, A.A., and S.S. Byushgens: K probleme popupatelnoi cili deneg.
Voprosi Konyunkturi 2 (1926), 151-171. English title: Conus, A.A.
and S.S. Buscheguennce, On the problem of the purchasing power of
money. The Problems of Economic Conditions, supplement to the
Economic Bulletin of the Conjuncture Institute 2 (1926), 151-171.

Kuiper, John: *MATOP: a generalized computer program for mathematical
operations.* Department of Economics, University of Ottawa, June 1974.

Lange, O.: The Determinateness of the Utility Function. *Review of
Economic Studies* 1 (1934), 218-224.

Laspeyres, E.: Hamburger Warenpreise 1850-1863. *Jahrbucher fur Nationalokonomie und Statistik* 3 (1864), 81 and 209.

————   Die Berechnung einer mittleren Waarenpreissteigerung.
Jahrbucher fur Nationalokonomie und Statistik (Jena) 16 (1871), 296-314.

Leacock, Stephen: Boarding-House Geometry. In *Literary Lapses*. Toronto:
McClelland and Stewart, 1910.

Leijonhufvud, A.: *On Keynesian Economics and the Economics of Keynes.*
Oxford University Press, 1968.

Leontief, W.: Composite Commodities and the Problem of Index Numbers.
Econometrica 4 (1936), 39-59.

Lerner, A.P.: A Note on the Theory of Price Index Numbers. *Review of
Economic Studies* (1935), 50-56.

Leser, C.E.V.: Forms of Engel Functions. *Econometrica* 31 (1963), 694-
703.

Little, I.M.D.: *A Critique of Welfare Economics.* Oxford University
Press, 1957.

Liviatan, Nissan, and Don Patinkin: On the Economic Theory of Price
Indices. *Economic Development and Cultural Change* 9 (1961), 501-536.

Lloyd, P.J.: Substitution effects and biases in non-true price indices.
American Economic Review, June 1975.

Machlup, Fritz: *Essays in Economic Semantics.* New York: W.W. Norton,

1967.

Malmquist, S.:   Index Numbers and Indifference Surfaces.   *Trabajos de Estadistica* 4 (1953), 209-242.

Malthus, Rev. T.R.:   Definitions in Political Economy, preceded by An Inquiry into the Rules Which Ought to Guide Political Economists in the Definition and Use of their Terms; with Remarks on the Deviations from these Rules in their Writings.   London, 1827.

Marris, Robin: *Economic Arithmetic.*   London: Macmillan, 1958.

Marshall, A.:   *Principles of Economics.*   London: 1st ed. 1890, 8th ed. 1946.

Mathur, P.N.:   Approximate Determination of Indifference Surfaces from Family Budget Data.   *International Economic Review* 5 (1964), 294-303.

Maunder, W.F.:   (ed.)   *Bibliography of Index Numbers.*   London: Athlone Press, 1970.

McKenzie, L.W.:   Demand Functions without a Utility Index.   *Review of Economic Studies* 24 (1957), 185-189.

Merilees, W.J.:   The case against Divisia index numbers as a basis in a social accounting system.   *Review of Income and Wealth* 17 (1971), 81-85.

Michael, Robert T.:   Variation across households in the rate of inflation.   *NBER Working Paper* No. 74 (March 1975).   Center for Economic Analysis of Human Behaviour and Social Institutions, Stanford, California.

Mishan, E.J.:   Theories of Consumers Behaviour: A Cynical View.   *Economica* 28 (February 1961), 1-11.

Mitchell, W.C.:   The Making and Using of Index Numbers.   Bureau of Labour Statistics, Washington 1921, Bulletin 284.

Mitzutani, K.:   New Formulae for Making Price and Quantity Index Numbers.   Chapter 27 in *Essays in Mathematical Economics in Honor of Oskar Morgenstern,* ed. by Martin Shubik.   Princeton University Press, 1967.

Morgenstern, Oskar: *On the Accuracy of Economic Observations.*   Princeton University Press, 1963.

————   Demand Theory Reconsidered.   *Quarterly Journal of Economics* 62 (February 1948), 165-201.   Reproduced in *The Evolution of Modern Demand Theory,* ed. by R.B. Ekelund *et al.* Lexington, Massachusetts: D.C. Heath and Co., 1972.

————   Thirteen Critical Points in Contemporary Economic Theory.

Working Paper No. 3 (April 1972), Department of Economics, New York University. *J. Econ. Literature* 10, (December 1972), 1163-1189.

Mudgett, B.D.: *Index Numbers*. New York: Wiley and Sons, 1951.

Muellbauer, J.: Prices and Inequality: the United Kingdom Experience. *Economic Journal* 84 (1974), 32-55.

────── The Political Economy of Price Indices. *Birkbeck Discussion Paper* No. 22 (March 1974).

────── Household Composition, Engel Curves and Welfare Comparisons between Households. *European Economic Review* 5 (August 1974).

────── Aggregation, Income Distribution and Consumer Demand. *Review of Economic Studies* 17, 4 (October 1975), 525-543.

Nataf, André, and René Roy: Remarques et suggestions relatives aux nombres-indices. *Econometrica* 16 (1948), 330-346.

National Council of Welfare: *Prices and the Poor: A Report by the National Council of Welfare on the Low-Income Consumer in the Canadian Marketplace*. Ottawa, April 1974.

Nicholson, J.L.: The Measurement of Quality Changes. *Economic Journal* 77 (1967), 512-530.

Paasche, H.: Uber die Preisentwickelung der letzten Jahre, nach den Hamburger Börsennotierungen. *Jahrbücher für Nationalökonomie und Statistik* (Jena) 23 (1874), 168-178.

Palgrave, R.H.I.: Currency and standard of value in England, France and India etc. *Memorandum to the Royal Commission on Depression of Trade and Industry,* Third Report, Appendix B, 1886.

Patinkin, D.: *Money, Interest, and Prices,* 2nd ed. New York: Harper and Row, 1965.

Pearce, I.F.: *A Contribution to Demand Analysis*. Oxford: The Clarendon Press, 1964.

Perroux, Francois: *Pouvoir et Economie*. Paris: Bordas, 1973.

Pfanzagl, J.: Zur Geschichte der Theorie des Lebenshaltungskostenindex. *Statistische Vierteljahresschrift* Bd. 8 (1955), 1-52.

Pfouts, R.W.: An Axiomatic Approach to Index Numbers. *Review of the International Statistical Institute,* Vol. 34, 2 (1966), 174-185.

Philips, L.: *Applied Consumption Analysis*. Amsterdam: North-Holland, 1974.

Pigou, A.C.: *The Economics of Welfare*. London: Macmillan, 1920.

Pollak, R.A.: The Theory of the Cost of Living Index. Discussion Paper No. 11, Office of Prices and Living Conditions, U.S. Bureau of Labor Statistics, Washington, D.C., 1971.

Prais, S.J.: Non-linear estimates of the Engel curves. *Review of Economic Studies* 20 (1952-53), 87-104.

Prais, S.J., and H.S. Houthakker: *The Analysis of Family Budgets*. Cambridge University Press, 1955.

Rajaoja, Vieno: A Study in the Theory of Demand Functions and Price Indexes. *Commentationes physico-mathematicae,* Societas Scientiarum Fennica (Helsinki) 21 (1958), 1-96.

Ricardo, David: Proposals for an Economical and Secure Currency (1816). In *The Works of David Ricardo,* ed. by J.R. McCulloch, 1852, p. 400.

Robinson, J.: *Economic Heresies*. London: Macmillan, 1971.

Roy, René: Les index économiques. *Revue d'Economie Politique* 41 (1927), 1251-1291.

——— *De l'utilité*. Actualités Scientifiques et Industrielles No. 930. Paris, 1942.

——— De la théorie de choix aux budgets de familles. *Econometrica* 17 (1949), 179-185.

Ruggles, Richard: Price Indices and International Price Comparisons. In *Ten Economic Studies in the Tradition of Irving Fisher*. New York: Wiley and Sons, 1967.

Ruist, Erik: Index Numbers, Theoretical Aspects. *International Encyclopaedia of the Social Sciences,* Vol. 7. New York, 1968.

Samuelson, P.A.: Some implications of 'linearity'. *Review of Economic Studies* 15 (1949), 88-90.

——— Evaluation of Real National Income. *Oxford Economic Papers,* New Series 2, 1 (1950), 1-29.

——— *Foundations of Economic Analysis*. Harvard University Press, 1947.

——— Remembrances of Frisch. *European Economic Review,* 1974.

——— Analytical Notes on International Real-Income Measures. *Economic Journal* (September 1974), 595-608.

Samuelson, P.A., and S. Swamy: Invariant Economic Index Numbers and
  Canonical Duality: Survey and Synthesis. *American Economic Review,*
  Vol. 64, 4 (1974), 566-593.

Sato, K.:   Ideal index numbers that almost satisfy factor reversal test.
  Review of Economics and Statistics 56 (1974), 549-552.

Schultz, H.:   A misunderstanding in index number theory: The true
  Konus condition on cost of living index numbers and its limitations.
  Econometrica (January 1939), p. 109.

Shephard, R.W.:   *Cost and Production Functions.* Princeton University
  Press, 1953.

————   *Theory of Cost and Production Functions.* Princeton University
  Press, 1970.

Schumpeter, Joseph A.:   *History of Economic Analysis.* Oxford University
  Press, 1954.

Scrope, G. Poulett: An Examination of the Bank Charter Question, with
  an inquiry into the nature of a just standard of value etc. London,
  1833.

Shubik, M.:   A Curmudgeon's Guide to Microeconomics. *Journal of
  Economic Literature,* June 1970.

Shubik, M. (editor):   *Studies in Mathematical Economics in Honor of
  Oskar Morgenstern.* Princeton University Press, 1967.

Slutsky, E.E.:   Sulla teoria del bilancio del consumatore. *Giornale
  degli Economisti* 51 (1915),' 1-26.   (Trans. by O. Ragusa: On the theory
  of the budget of the consumer.   In *Readings in Price Theory,* ed. by
  G.J. Stigler and K.E. Boulding.   Ch. 2, 27-65.   Chicago: Irwin,
  Inc., 1952.)

Staehle, Hans: A Development of the Economic Theory of Price Index
  Numbers. *Review of Economic Studies* (1935), 163-188.

————   Annual Survey of Statistical Information: Family Budgets.
  Econometrica 2 (October 1934), 349-362.

Stigler, G.J.:   (chairman)   Report on the Price Statistics of the
  Federal Government, National Bureau of Economic Research, General
  Series, No. 73.   New York, 1961.

Stone, Richard: The Role of Measurement in Economics. Cambridge University
  Press, 1951.

————   Linear Expenditure Systems and Demand Analysis; an Application
  to the Pattern of British Demand. *Economic Journal* 64 (1954), 511-524.

———— Quantity and Price Indexes in National Accounts. Published by OEEC, Paris, 1956.

Stone, Richard, assisted by D.A. Rowe, W.J. Corlett, R. Hurstfield, and M. Potter. *The Measurement of Consumer's Expenditure and Behaviour in the United Kingdom, 1920-1938,* Vol. 1. Cambridge University Press, 1966.

Stuvel, G.: A New Index Number Formula. *Econometrica* 25 (1957), 123-131.

Subramanian, S.: On a Certain Conclusion of Frisch's. *Journal of the American Statistical Association* 29 (1934), 316-317.

Swamy, S.: Consistency of Fisher's Tests. *Econometrica* 33 (1965), 619-623.

Theil, H.: *Economics and Information Theory.* Amsterdam: North Holland, 1967.

———— On the geometry and the numerical approximation of cost of living and real income indices. *De Economist* 116 (1968), 677-689.

———— A New Index Number Formula. *Review of Economics and Statistics* (1973), 498-502.

Tornquist, L.: The Bank of Finland consumption price index. *Bank of Finland Monthly Bulletin* 10 (1936), 1-8.

U.S. Congress: Joint Economic Committee, *Government Price Statistics.* Hearings before the subcommittee on Economic Statistics. 87th Congress, 1st Session. *Report of the Price Statistics Review Committee,* Washington, D.C., Part 1, 5-99. Government Printing Office, 1961.

Ulmer, M.J.: *The Economic Theory of Cost of Living Index Numbers.* Columbia University Press, 1949.

Vartia, Yrjö O.: Relative changes and economic indices (in Finnish). A Licentiate Thesis, Department of Statistics, University of Helsinki, 1974.

———— Ideal log-change index numbers. *Discussion Paper* No. 2 (June 1976). The Research Institute of the Finnish Economy (ETLA). Forthcoming in the *Scandinavian Journal of Statistics.*

———— Fisher's Five-Tined Fork and Other Quantum Theories of Index Numbers. *Discussion Paper* No. 3 (June 1976). The Research Institute of the Finnish Economy (ETLA).

Ville, J.: Sur les conditions d'existence d'une orphelimite totale et d'un indice du niveau des prix. Annales de l'Université de Lyon, 1946.

The Existence Conditions of a Total Utility Function. *Review of Economic Studies* 19 (1951-52), 128-132.

Viner, J.: The Utility Concept in Value Theory and its Critics. *Journal of Political Economy* 33 (1925), 369-387, 638-659.

Voeller, J.: Theorie des Preis- und Lebenshaltungskostenindex. *Dissertation,* Karlsruhe, 1974.

Wald, A.: Zür Theorie der Preisindexziffern. *Zeitschrift für Nationalökonomie* 8 (1937), 179-219.

————   A New Formula for the Index of the Cost of Living. *Econometrica* 7, 4 (1939), 319-335.

Walras, L.: *Eléments d'économie pure.* Paris: 1st ed. 1874, 5th ed. 1926.

Walsh, C.H.: *The Measurement of General Exchange-Value.* New York: Macmillan, 1901.

Weintraub, E. Roy: *General Equilibrium Theory.* London: Macmillan, 1974.

Wicksell, Knut: *Lectures on Political Economy. Volume II: Money.* London: Routledge, 1935.

Wold, H.O.A.: A synthesis of pure demand analysis. *Skandinavisk Aktuarietidskrift* 26 (1943), 85-118, 221-263; ibid. 27 (1944), 69-120.

Wright, Georg Henrik von: *The Logic of Preference.* Edinburgh University Press, 1963.

Additions to bibliography:

Dahrendorf, Ralf: The 1974 Reith Lectures 'The New Liberty: survival and justice in a changing world', 4th Lecture 'On Difference' reproduced in *The Listener,* 5 December 1974, 724-726.

Tintner, Gerhard: Homogeneous Systems in Mathematical Economics. *Econometrica* 16, 4 (October 1948), 273-294.

Anderson, O.: Mehr Vorsicht mit Indexzahlen. *Allg. Statist. Arch.* 33 (1949), 472-479.

Paige, Deborah and Gottfried Bombach: *A Comparison of National Output and Productivity of the United Kingdom and the United States.* Joint Study by the Organisation for European Economic Co-operation and the Department of Applied Economics, University of Cambridge. OEEC, Paris, 1959.

Benedetti, Carlo: Teorie e tecniche dei numeri indici. *Metron* 22, 1-2 (December 1962), 3-97.

————   Ricerche su un tipo generalizzato di indice del costo della vita. *Metron* 27, 3-4(December 1969), 3-40.

————   Vecchi e tradizionali indici dei prezzi ricondotti a moderni indici funzionali a costante utilità. *Metron* 30, 1-4(December 1972), 1-20.

Vartia, Yrjö O.: *Relative Changes and Index Numbers*. Helsinki: The Research Institute of the Finnish Economy, 1976.

Eichhorn, Wolfgang and Joachim Voeller: *Theory of the Price Index*. Berlin: Springer-Verlag, 1976.